PROFESSOR BLOOMER'S NO-NONSENSE READING PROGRAM:

A SIMPLIFIED PHONETIC
APPROACH
TO
READING, WRITING, AND SPELLING

TEACHERS MANUAL
Volume 1
Fifth Edition

RICHARD H. BLOOMER, ED.D., M. S.
Emeritus Professor
The University of Connecticut

All rights reserved. No part of this book may be reproduced, scanned, or distributed in any printed or electronic form without permission, in any printed or electronic form. Please do not participate in or encourage piracy of copyrighted material in violation of United States and International copyright laws

Copyright 1956, 1968, 1973, 2002, 2017.

IBSN 978-0-9997244-2-2

Beginning Reading, Writing, Spelling, Home-Schooling, First Grade, Kindergarten, Education,

If you want someone to learn something, teach it to them
　　　　　　　　　　E. L. Thorndike, 1946

Reviews for Professor Bloomer's Work

Professor Bloomer's Aesop's Fables

What a wonderful collection of stories for children to learn from, to experience the art of the story, and to expand their knowledge and understanding. Children have been reading and relating to these stories for generations … Dr. Bloomer has the right idea … he has captured the essence of comprehension: provide stories that children can relate to, stories that have meaning for them, stories that bring the culture to them at a level they can understand. Further, this collection of stories is able to provide a broad basis of instruction of thoughts, ideas, vocabulary, all set in a rich background for discussion, for problem solving and for exploration of feelings and opinions … and it is based on neuroscience …I highly recommend this text for teachers, for reading specialist, and for special educators … well done, Dr. Bloomer!   P.P .Rhode Island

I love Dr. Bloomer's approach to learning both in this reading program and in his spelling program (also available on Amazon). He looks beyond instructing to meet minimum educational standards and tests to actually helping students develop practical problem-solving skills that they can use throughout their lives—he wants to make better people, not just better students. The idea to use Aesop's Fables as a basis for reading comprehension for young students is genius ☺. These stories are simple and straightforward, but also thought-provoking, generating discussion of important moral and ethical concepts. As a context for reading comprehension, they engage students' imagination and feelings, which further helps to reinforce the learning process.   C.C. Florida

Professor Bloomer's No-Nonsense Spelling Program

5.0 out of 5 starsFive Stars
ByPatricia A. Pezzullo on September 1, 2015
Format: Paperback|Verified Purchase
excellent …just excellent! Thank you, Dr. Bloomer …

Professor Bloomer's No-Nonsense Spelling Program

Finally! Dr. Bloomer takes spelling beyond memorizing a list of vocabulary words to a more holistic level! Professor Bloomer's program is a fundamental learning process that not only teaches thousands of words, but gives students transferable skills to successfully improve reading, writing, comprehension, memorization, vocabulary, and general problem solving. If you are a dedicated teacher, tutor, or home-schooling parent, this program will help your student excel in spelling and other language arts. Your student will learn how to learn, which helps them become more independent learners and ultimately increases their capacity to learn and succeed. If you want to teach spelling, try Professor Bloomer's practical, step-by-step approach and reap the surprising benefits!

WW-II Chronicles

Fantastic story telling. Wish a publishing house would pick it up to do it the honor of the editing and design the story deserves. The magical voice will take you far and help you ……… experience WWII from the bottom.

One of the best reads ever. Short, concise, punchy, Bloomer's coming of age while carrying an M-1 would make a great action movie. It's full of action both in and out of the trenches.

A Boy' Life;
I had the pleasure of working with RHB at UConn for several years. This is a great book, written from the heart. If you know Dick, you will REALLY enjoy reading this!

This is a book by a born storyteller. It weaves and wanders through times past as engagingly as the early English novelists. Bloomer's voice is both tender and sardonic and a world is recreated in his words. I'm very happy to have this in my collection and want to start the follow-up volume, "World War II Chronicles" as soon as I can.

Books by Richard H. Bloomer

Professor Bloomer's No-Nonsense Beginning Phonetic Reading Series
    Basic Phonetic Reading, Teacher's Guide, Vol. 1.
    Basic Phonetic Reading, Student's Learning Book, Vol. 2.
    First Phonetic Reader, Teacher's Guide, Vol. 3.
    First Phonetic Reader, Student's Learning Book. Vol. 4.
    Second Phonetic Reader, Teacher's Guide Vol 5.
    Second Phonetic Reader, Student's learning Book, Vol. 6.

Coming:
    Complex Phonetics Teacher's Guide, Vol. 7.
    Complex Phonetics Student's Learning Book, Vol;. 8

Professor Bloomer's No-Nonsense Elementary Education Books
    No-Nonsense Spelling Program
    No-Nonsense Handwriting Program
    Bloomer's Aesop's Fables

Coming:
    No-Nonsense Vocabulary Improvement Program

Bloomer's Developmental Neuropsychological Assessment Series
    Individual Response Speed Vol. 1.
    Individual Short Term Memory, Vol. 2..
    Reading Skills Diagnostic Test, Vol. 3.

Coming:
    Assessing Natural Memory, Contiguity and Similarity,Vol. 4.
    Artificial Memory 1. Sequencing and OrderVol. 5.
    Artificial Memory 2. Purposeful Association, Vol. 6
    Complex Stimulus Hierarchical Processes, Vol. 7.
    Connotative Meaning, Limbic Processes Vol. 8
    Sharpening up Old Tools, Vol. 9.

Autobiographical
    A Boy's Life
    World War II Chronicles: A View of War From the Bottom

Acknowledgments

This work is hardly mine alone. It rests on the work of many scholars and scientists reaching back into antiquity.

The ancient Phoenicians knew that by mastering Letter/sounds and putting them together to make spoken words, readers could obtain meaning from written words. Once the visual word is encoded into speech, meaning or understanding is a separate and very different set of mental processes contingent upon the learner's prior experiences.

At Teachers College, Edward L. Thorndike and Irving Lorge shaped my scientific attitude. Robert S. Woodworth never let me forget that there is an "Orgamism" between the "Stimulus" and the "Response." Percival Symonds provided encouraging mentorship and laboratory space for my early experiments in human learning.

I wish to thank the folks at Central Institute for the Deaf, for simplifying the standard phonetic alphabet to make it much simpler and more useful for students to learn their letter/sounds

All research tracks need an initial stimulus. Mine was provided by my friend Myron Woolman, whose early case studies in teaching adult reading prompted me to research and refine those seminal ideas into a systematic, integrated language teaching program for children.

Much credit is due to the Olivetti Underwood Corporation who funded our original Reading/Typing program from whence these readers were born

Most important, an exceptional teacher, Frances Little, who adopted the first edition of this integrated language program, had the courage to go against the educational trends and her peers, and whose pupils never failed to succeeded in reading during her twenty-seven years as a first-grade teacher.

To Dr. Ann Marie Bernaza-Haase, who was instrumental in shaping my musings into the Reading/Typing Program and developed many of the stories and workbook materials that made our phonetic readers possible

To my supportive partner, Jan Maya Schold, who gives me the space to think and create and an occasional jog to spur me on and chipped in many of her precious hours to find and correct my many mistakes

Many of the illustrations were done by our wonderful local artist and calligrapher, Kathy LePack

Much Credit must be given to Dover publications and the Nova Development company of California for generous permission to use their royalty free images.

Within my personal experience. my grandfather Hermon Hutcheson drilled into my wnadring preadolescent mind his mantra "There ain't no such word as can't."

Last, and perhaps most important, was my own wicked step mother, Marguerite Barnes Bloomer, who with boundless patience first taught me "how" to learn. She also taught me, that "Learning is not fun." Learning is hard work; it is the accomplishment that is rewarding.

"Literacy is the most important factor in building and preserving our civilization, and teaching children to read is the most important task of our schools. We perform this task clumsily and with great waste of labor and time. Even at the end of eight years many of our public school pupils cannot be said to read; yet eight months ought to suffice." (Leonard Bloomfield, 1942)

PROFESSOR BLOOMER'S NO-NONSENSE READING PROGRAM:

Preface to the fifth edition

I first wrote this program initially in 1952 as a guide for my students for a remedial reading clinic as a part of a reading methods class. We had sufficient success with that approach that school principals asked us to return year after year. One teacher used the guide for her first grade class and had excellent results The present program was written adapted for the classroom from that original guide in the academic year 1956-57.

The teacher who first used Professor Bloomer's No-Nonsence Reading Program as a first grade classroom reading method back in 1957, every single child she ever taught, achieved above second grade level, for her whole twenty-seven year teaching career. Another school using this program in addition to averaging one full grade level above their peers, taught using a popular standard commercal curriculum, reduced referrals for Special Education by 65% and the positive effects of Professor Bloomer's No-Nonsense Reading Program lasted at least until grade seven.

In our clinic at UConn we have used Professor Bloomer's program successfully with dyslexics, children with learning diabilities, speech difficulties, brain damage, and ADHD. During the intervening years we have found that Professor Bloomers No-Nonsense Reading Program works as well with non-English speakers in Latin America and China as long as their instructor speaks English

Over the last sixty years the quality of public school children's reading has diminished steadily. The many "Reading Plans," periodically put forward are acts of desperation, and have little effect on this downward slide in children's reading skills. It is this same desperation felt by the parents who bring their children to me for help that has prompted this fifth edition of Professor Bloomer's No-Nonsense Reading Program for Young Learners.

Professor Bloomer's No-Nonsense Reading Program is designed based upon the neuro-science of learning as a step by step plan for parents and teachers to help children through the stages of early reading. The program is specifically focused toward reading independence and developing the learners abilities to figure out new words on their own. Once these skills are mastered the learner is ready to explore the wide range of learning possibilities offered by additional schooling

RHB
Wilimantic, CT
2017

Introduction to Professor Bloomer's No-Nonsense Reading Program for Young Learners

Good reading skill is the most useful tool our can schools provide our children. Reading enables learning in all other subjects. When a reader is skilled, reading is the most effective method of communication. It is faster, more accurate, more stable and less expensive than any other means of communication. Reading is the basis of a free and democratic society. It is small wonder that a major effort of educators is in attempts to improve the teaching of reading. In spite of all this effort, between thirty and fifty percent of public school children still fail to master reading at the most basic reading level.

Learning to read with the right curriculum is not a difficult task. Professor Bloomer's No-Nonsense Reading Program, is an excellent beginning reading program, a simple, scientifically organized, phonetic method; a reading program designed to be flexible enough to accept children's differences. Using Professor Bloomer's No-Nonsense Reading Program a consistent patient teacher who will adapt to children's differences will have close to one hundred percent success.

Why does the United States have a reading problem?
The ancient inventors of the alphabet knew that by mastering letter/sounds and a technique for putting them together to make spoken words, readers could easily obtain meaning from written words. This process was called Phonetics. It was and still is, the most successful method for teaching reading for more than three millennia.

Around the turn of the Twentieth century the United States ranked first among nations in literacy. Much of this was due to teaching reading by Spelling and by phonetic methods. The Progressive Educators shifted the reading teaching model from an emphases of building words from letters or phonetic elements into teaching memorization of the "Whole Word." They began to emphasize the negatives of English phonetic system; and to use those few wierd non-phonetic anomalies in the English language, to try to convince themselves, and others that English reading could be taught better by the "Whole Word" method. In reality the Whole Word method did not work very well, and the nation's reading ability tumbled on a downward spiral wherever the Whole Word method is adopted. As a result the United States has fallen from first place in world literacy to seventeenth.

Teaching Reading Today
With Progressive Educators seeking a magic key to effortless learning, modern reading curricula have become numerous and complicated. Every few years, reading professionals seem to discover a new and "revolutionary" solution to America's reading ills.

Progressive Educators have invented numerous patches to shore up the Whole Word Method in an attempt to stem the increasingly vast percentage of children's failures. Teachers, frantic to produce good readers, are ready to try anything new. Chief, among these patches was the invention of even less efficient Analytic Phonics, and Phonemic Awareness. These and other patches have only succeeded only in over-complicating the reading teaching task beyond anyones ability to comprehend. From an historic perspective the only things that are really new in these "new solutions to the reading problem are the name applied to the methods and their authors. These methods simply recycle old, failed ideas under shiny new names.

Political candidates periodically promise to institute accountability, or to throw more money at education to solve this reading crisis. To make things more complicated, modern reading curricula try to serve multiple masters. Besides attempting to teach reading, modern curricula endeavor to teach social skills, diversity, understanding, thinking skills, problem solving, emotional balance and more. While each of these goals maybe laudable, reading itself gets lost in the complexity.

Despite this confusing array of incentives, methods, curricula, goals, and government initiatives, the reading ability of America's youth has continually spiraled in declined over the last century. Between thirty and fifty percent of American children currently fail to master their minimal State's Basic Level reading skills. Educational book publishers welcome and foster each new magical teaching fad, for it means more new books and materials to be sold. The great tragedy is most modern day teachers, trained only in the Whole Word method, are unaware of the simplicity and much higher success rate of the phonetic reading methods.

Reading Demystified

Let's take a positive stance and peel away the commercial hype and the educational mythology from the complicated methodological patchwork of the classroom reading teacher and look at the affirmative potential for constructing a true phonetic method for teaching English reading in the light of well-established scientific principles.

Phonetic reading is basically is learning the sounds that relate to forty-four visual signals (Letter/sounds) into mental images of a sequence of these letter/sounds into words. To simplify the English phonetics, Professor Bloomer has broken the phonetic system into two parts. Simple phonetics, the five short vowels and the simple consonants.
To be able to read, a person must be able to:

(1) Recognize the 25 visual signals,
(2) convert them into mental images of sounds, and
(3) sequence these sounds left to right to make words.

Once the learner can perform these processes automatically, he can read independently. The rest is practice and learning the fine points of the more complex phonetics of our language. Professor Bloomer's No-Nonsence Reading Program efficiently focuses on these simple essential goals direclty and defers more complex phonetic skills until the learner reading skills are more mature.

What's Unique about Professor Bloomer's Reading Program?
In contrast to most modern commercial reading programs, Professor Bloomer's phonetic program is based on long-established scientifically tested learning principles. It is unique in adapting these principles to a young learner's limited memory span.

Phonetics versus Phonics
Phonetics and Phonics are completely different models of teaching reading. Professor Bloomer's reading program is a phonetic program which builds or constructs words from it's letter/sounds. It is not a "phonics" program which tears down the words into their component letter/sound parts and then tries to re-build them back into words. Phonics was invented by educators to try to stem the flood of non-readers caused by lack of letter/sounds in the "Whole Word" method. Analytic phonics had to start with the whole word to maintain the integrity of the "Whole Word" concept. Phonics begins by teaching children to memorize whole words, then they learn to deconstruct, to break down, or analyze the words into it's component parts, letters or syllables, Then they try to match the letter or syllables with some previously learned sounds from another word, and finally to guess, or 'encode' the torn apart letters back into a word. This is a complicated set of cognitive proceses which is difficult for immature first grade minds to capture.

What is Phonetic reading?
Professor Bloomer's Phonetics on the other hand, starts by teaching children the simple twenty-five letter/sounds, one at a time, and then teaching children the easy process of putting these letter sounds together, from left too right, so children make their own words. Professor Bloomer uses the most efficient phonetic design called Constructive Synthetic Phonetics.

Constructive synthetic phonetics
Conatructive synthesis is the mental process of building words from their letter sounds. The Constructive Synthetic Phonetic model based on the psychology of learning, potentially has the highest success rate of all phonics or phonetic systems. The important factor in constructive phonetics is introducing the learner to only one new letter form with its sound at one time. The learner is taught how to combine each new letter/sound with the previous learned letter/sounds to construct words. Constructive phonetics learners read, write, and spell every new word they learn. Limiting new learning to a single new letter/sound memory is never overloaded, and the learner easily masters reading, writing, and spelling. The learner's memory span also grows with repeated practice across several days.

It works like this: Before the children are introduced to books or sight words the children begin learning the letters with their sounds one at a time. The names of the letters are not used, each letter is identified by it's sound. Thus the children will learn the letter A as its short sound /a/ as in FAT) The next lesson will teach the letter T by it's sound /T/ and begin to construct the word "AT and TAT.

The next lesson, letter/sound /S/. allows the children to build AS and SAT. Teaching the letter/sound /M/ allows the learner to construct AM, MAT, MAST, MAM, and SAM. The number of new words grows nearly geometrically with each new letter/sound combination.

Sounds

Professor Bloomer's reading program follows the Phoenician model. Learners are taught to call letter forms by their sound names one at a time. (for example, the /m/ in 'mat' and the /b/ in 'bat'). Each new sound is combined with previous learned letter/sounds to construct words. Note that sounds or letter/sounds in the teachers manual are written between two slanted lines, so that you can distinguish a sound from an ordinary letter.

Memory

The average First grade beginning reader has a limited memory capacity for remembering new information. Usually, first graders can remember only three sounds at a time, or a little less than one word. If we try to introduce more new information than the learner's memory can hold, he will begin to feel stressed, frustrated, and anxious. Professor Bloomer resolves the memory problem, and avoids developing learner's anxiety, by teaching only one single new letter/sound at a time. Professor Bloomer's Reading Program gradually improves the learner's memory capacity as he masters reading and spelling while protecting learners from stress and anxiety.

Capital Letters

Similarly, in Professor Bloomer's No-Nosense Reading Program only the capital letter form is used in teaching because it is larger, easier to see, and write, and much less confusing than small letters or cursive forms. Further, using capital forms allows us to avoid learning the confusing capitalization rules until the next level when the learner is more skilled and we introduce the small letter forms.

Consistency

Consistency makes learning easier. In Professor Bloomers Reading Program we consistently call letters by their letter/sounds. The alphabetic name is never used. This prevents the learner from having to make a choice as to how to pronounce a letter shape and thus simplifying the process. In English, letter forms usually—but not always—correspond to sounds. We postpone learning these more tortuous exceptions to regular phonemic forms until the second level of Professor Bloomer's program so each word in this program is easy to read. Our learners develop skills at decoding before meeting the dreaded English phonetic foibles of these complex forms.

Language:

Word knowledge is a basic tool for thinking. Words are the carriers of meaning. It is difficult to think about things you read if you don't have the words to know what to call thhings, Most Whole Word reading programs limit children's language to the most common words. Children are taught only words they already are familiar with and thus their thinking is limited to the mondain. Professor Bloomer believes in increasing children's vocabulary and opening learners to new and unusual words and ideas. Phonetics gives the learner the tool to figure out any new word. The words in this program are controlled only by the letter/sounds the children have learned. Learning each new letter/sound brings with it dozens of interesting words, unusual words, even old time archaic words, all designed to open the child's mind beyond his present levels.

Applications

Constructive synthetic Phonetics has tested numerous times. It has always been more successful in every single comparison with commercial reading programs. It has a wide range of applications in teaching language skills. We used this program at the A.J. Papinakou Center for Special Education at the Universdity of Connecticut for a wide variety of learners with reading and learning problems. Using a constructive synthetic phonetics reding/typing program children from lower SES and Bilingual children finished the program with test scores averaging one to two years above grade level, and reading on a level equal to middle class children. Second grade children tested at 6th grade in spelling The Special Education referrals in that school were reduced by 2/3rds when compared with children taught by a popular Whole Word method. This constructive synthesis model program has been used in both Latin America and China to teach English to native speakers. The model itself is applicable to a wide variety of learning problems.

Case Study

One day, an upset mother came into my office with her son Roy, a second grader. She explained the problem:

"Roy was doing so wonderfully last year in first grade. He got all 'A's. But this year, in second grade, he has a lot of trouble with reading. Now he tells me he hates school and doesn't want to go. The teacher tells me Roy is beginning to act out and has temper tantrums in class. I don't know what to do. Roy's getting so difficult."

I had a number of different graded reading books on my shelves. "Go pick a book," I said to Roy.

He chose a book, a first-grade reader, brought it over, sat down, and proceeded to read it perfectly.

"That's wonderful," I said.

"Now let's try this book," I suggested, picking another first-grade reader.

"I don't know that book," said Roy.

"That's OK," I said. "You should know some of the words anyway."

He opened the book. The first word was 'The.' Roy didn't respond. After several seconds, he said,

"I don't know that one."

"That's strange," I thought. "Can he really not read 'The,' or is he just being stubborn?"

"Tell me this word," I said, pointing to the word 'The' in the book he had just read for me.

"That word says 'the.'"

"Good, now what is this word?" I asked, pointing to 'The' in the second book.

"I don't know," Roy said, visibly frustrated.

"Better try another approach, "I thought, "Do you like school in second grade?" I asked.

"Hate it."

"What's your worst subject?"

"Reading."

"That's strange. You read your book so well.'

"Too many words to learn, and not enough pictures," Roy explained.

After a few more questions, I finally figured out that Roy was a bright child who had been taught by the "Whole Language story" method. He was memorizing stories and using the pictures to cue his memory. In second grade, the stories became too long and there were not enough pictures to cue his memory. His memory, though excellent, was overloaded. Anxiety, school avoidance and temper tantrums resulted. Although no one would suspect, Roy could not read at all.

When I tested Roy, I found he had no notion that letters and sounds corresponded. He didn't even know that letters were related to sounds. In this sense he was fortunate. He had nothing to unlearn. We did not have to combat incorrectly learned letter/sounds, confused reading processes, and the anxiety that often affects the poor reader.

I taught Roy the Letter 'A' by its corresponding sound /A/. Then, I taught '/T/' and showed him how to write the words 'AT' and 'TAT.' He learned the letter/sound /M/ and we built the words 'AM,' 'MAM,' 'TAM,' and 'MAT.' When he learned the letter/Letter/sound /S/ he suddenly got it.

"Oh, this one says 'SAM,' and this is 'SAT.'" Roy announced proudly.

Roy had passed the crucial barrier--understanding the process by which words are built. It is this process that allows the learner to read new words. It removes the excessive memory demands of memorizing each word. From there, it took only three more sessions with this exceptional boy to go through the simple Letter/sounds and practice putting them together into words.

Roy was off and running. His mother was delighted. His bad behavior diminished. He spent much of his time puzzling out the words in books. As a bright and eager young man, Roy had the simple tools to solve most of his remaining reading challenges by himself.

How Well Does It Work?
You may be wondering what results Professor Bloomer's Reading Program can produce. In fact, this program has been used successfully for more than 55 years, with classrooms and with individual learners, including children in special education, bilingual children, with adolescents and adults who could not read. For example, one first-grade teacher in New York used the program for her whole teaching career. Every single one of her learners for 27-years tested above the average for all other first-grade classes in her school system.

In a follow up study comparing children taught by Constructive Synthetic Phonetics with those taught by the standard Progressive Education whole Word curriculum for the first two years of school.

Professor Bloomer's No-Nonsense Reading Program

When they reached seventh grade, children taught by Dr Bloomer Constructive Synthetic Phonetic method, at seventh grade, averaged at least two years ahead in reading, spelling, and language arts than those children taught by a popular standard commercial Word Method curriculum. Similar results have been found for many learners from New England to Texas to Alaska. Standardized test scores also show higher reading scores for learners taught using Professor Bloomer's program. We have successfully used the program as an introduction to English reading, writing, and spelling for both children and adults who are non-English speakers

By learning the various language skills—reading, spelling, writing, and speaking—together in a single lesson, instead of in separate lessons, the learner not only acquires individual skills but does so more effectively and in a meaningful contex

General Teaching Principles

In each unit, the procedures have been organized along the following general principles. They are restated here so that you may become familiar with them.

Connect sounds and letters

1. Use only the sound of the letter. Do not use the alphabet name for the letter/sound. See p[ronuncuation Key below

SIMPLE PHONETICS PRONUNCIATION KEY BY LESSON ORDER

1.	/A/	as in fat	9.	/D/	as in dog	17.	/V/	as in vest
2.	/T/	as in tap	10.	/N/	as in nut	18.	/K/	as in kick
3.	/S/	as in sat	11.	/U/	as in nut	19.	/B/	as in bad
4.	/M/	as in mad	12.	/H/	as in hat	20.	/O/	as in top
5.	/R/	as in ran	13.	/J/	as in jet	21.	/Y/	as in yet
6.	/G/	as in good	14.	/L/	as in like	22.	/P/	as in pot
7.	/F/	as in fat	15.	/C/	as in cut	23.	/E/	as in net
8.	/W/	as in wet	16.	/I/	as in insist	24.	/Z/	as in zoo
						25.	/X/	as in tax

2. Have the learner write and say every letter/sound and word as he sounds them out. This method forces the learner to use all three senses of speaking hearing, and motor kinesthet ics for each response. The more senses he uses in making answers, the better he will learn.

3. When you introduce a new letter/sound sound, underline the letter/sound the first few times you show it. This method ensures that the learner will know which letter/sound in a word has the sound attached to it.

4. Point to each letter/sound (or have the learner point) as it is being sounded out. Gradually eliminate this habit as the learner becomes a better reader.

Professor Bloomer's No-Nonsense Reading Program

5. From the beginning of the training, be sure that the learner learns not only the sound of the new letter/sound, but also how to put that sound together with other sounds into words. This method helps the learner become more independent in reading. Knowing how to put sounds together into words is almost as important as knowing the sound sounds them selves.

Writing

1. Always have the learner write all words and sounds in **capital form** only. By using a single consistent letter forms, the learner is less likely to become confused. Consistency always helps the learner.

2. Have the learner practice writing the letter several times while you guide the strokes verbally, or physically guide him if necessary.

3. Always put the letter/sounds together from left to right and top to bottom. If the learner confronts words only in this direction, she is less likely to reverse letter/sound shapes such as 'S' and 'Z' or become confused about the sequence of the sounds in a word.

Encourage the learner

1. Let the learner try. The more effort he puts into the task, the greater the benefit and learn ing. Success is sweetest when the learner has achieved it himself. Too much help teaches the learner to feel helpless. Success achieved on his own leads to greater independence.

2. Always tell the learner when he is right. Acknowledging his correct answers helps the learner feel successful and encourages him to try harder.

3. Even if the learner makes an error, point out any parts of his answer that are correct before explaining any parts that are wrong. For example, if a learner says "BAT" for "PAT," explain that he has most of the word right. Tell him that "B" is much like "P" in sound and shape. Be sure that he knows the difference between the two. Ask him if he would like to try again.

4. Give gentle corrections. Teach the learner that everyone makes errors. Try to correct the mistakes without making the learner feel bad. Strong corrections usually make the learner anxious and likely to make even more errors. They can harm a learner's whole reading career. A learner will perform better if he is not afraid of what the teacher will say if the learner gets an answer wrong.

5. Encourage the learner to give an answer. Have him give those sounds in the word he knows. even if he is unsure or needs help. A learner who finally works out an answer, even if he needed hints, feels more successful than someone who gets the answer from the teacher or gives no answer or gives up entirely. He also learns that he should work at errors, not ignore them.

6. If he still doesn't have the complete answer, give him only the missing parts. In that case, be sure that the learner repeats the whole answer after you. Try to get the learner to build the answer from the parts. Be sure also to tell him "That's good" or "That's right" after his repetition, for in truth he has made a correct response, and you should always acknowledge right answers.

7. If the learner has continual trouble adjust the task to fit the learner's abilities, until the l earner can fit the task.

8. Consistency and patience are the teacher's most important qualities.

Pacing Lessons Builds Memory

1. Teach and review reading several times throughout the day and across several days rather than in a single session. A young learner's attention span is short, and she will prob ably become bored with long lessons. To review, use games or connect reading with other work. In this way learners recognize that reading is a part of life, not restricted to a particu lar period of the day. Spacing out the lessons also stimulates the learner's memory and en sures long- term memory storage.

2. Ask the learner for the meaning of any words he sounds out. Ask him to use each word in a sentence. This procedure tends to stop him from guessing the word and helps him learn how to put words together. In this way the learner comes to realize that the words he is reading have meaning.

3. At the beginning of each lesson, announce how long the session will last and what it will cover. Thus the learners will be able to measure what they have accomplished. Similarly, at the end of each lesson, give a summary.

4. Keep a chart to show the learner his progress.

5. Gradually, as the learner masters more words, increase the number of words in each lesson—and therefore the difficulty. But do not move too fast. A gradual increase prevents the faster learner from being bored and at the same time challenges all learners.

6. Schedule reading lessons every other day or spaced throughout the day, to give the brain time to make connections. Spacing is good for building the memory too!

Mental Processing in reading: Reading is not "natural." It does not just pop out of ones head as some claim. On the other hand, with the right curriculum, achieving independent reading is not a difficult task. Good reading is the result of systematic mental processes applied to the written word, to convert thoise visual signals into spoken words. Our goal is to teach our learners the most efficient mental p[rocesses for independent reading so our readers will be able to confront any unknown word and come up with an acceptable pronounciation independently and with no assistance. For this purpose each lesson will use exercises of the same format, each of these fourteen exercises will add a component to the learners ability to read the english language

Who can teach Professor Bloomer's No-Nonsense Reading Program?
Anyone who speaks English. The procedure for each lesson is spelled out in easy to follow directions. The key is patience and consistency. Impatience induces anxiety in both teacher and pupil and slows the learning dramatically. Inconsistency confuses the child and makes the learning problem unclear. If you are impatient, or inconsistent, find someone else to teach.

Assess yourself as a teacher

This book was written for the teacher, parent, or other concerned adult who is responsible for the education of a child. If you are reading this book, you probably want to use it to help a child learn. Before you begin, it's a good idea to assess whether you are likely to be an effective teacher. Not everyone will make a good teacher. The questions below can help you decide whether to attempt this role. If you yourself are unlikely to be an effective teacher, you can probably find a tutor who can do a good job.

Do you have time to teach—at least 20-40 minutes a day?	Do you think your learner is, or could be, an Einstein?
Can you set aside a regular time for teaching two or three days a week?	Do you feel your learner must keep up with his class?
Do you have a positive attitude?	Are you afraid your learner will fall behind his peers?
Will your learner do what you ask?	Do you have a temper?
Are you a patient person?	Are you frustrated doing the same thing over and over?
If you answer no or maybe to any of the questions above, consider hiring a tutor	If you answer yes to any of the questions above, consider hiring a tutor.

I have found that untrained tutors are often more likely to succeed with Professor Bloomer's methods and produce good results than are many Whole Word Method trained teachers, who often get bored and want to have fun or attempt to find a quicker or easier way.

Who can learn from Professor Bloomer's No-Nonsense Reading Program?
Anyone who does not read and write English. We have successfully taught regular classrooms, remedial readers, LD's, ADHD's, autistic children, children with Asperger's, children with mental retardation, and children and adults with brain damage. Because of it's simplicity Professor Bloomer's program has been a rapid method for adults and children speaking other languages to learn to read, write, and speak English. It is best used with young school aged children, beginning their learning careers, and before they have learned poor habits which may interfere with learning to read and write.

Teaching Professor Bloomer's No-Nonsense Reading Program
The method is easy to administer. The teacher should speak clearly because your students will be imitating your language patterns. The directions are easy to follow. Each lesson must follow the same pattern of directions. As you are teaching reading, you are also teaching an efficient process for learning other things. We do not want a new or different pattern to interfere with your learner's progress. Go as slowly as you need to be sure your learner has learned each lesson before going on to the next. You are never in a hurry.

Contents

Introduction	i
Why does the United States have a reading problem	i
Teaching Reading Today	i
Reading Demystified	i
What's Unique about this Reading Program?	iii
Phonetics versus Phonics	iii
What is Phonetic reading?	iii
Constructive synthetic phonetics	iii
Sounds.	iv
Memory.	iv
Capital Letters.	iv
Consistency	iv
Language	iv
Applications	v
Case Study	v
How well does it work?	vi
General Teaching Principles	vii
Connect Sounds and Letters	vii
Writing	viii
Encourage the Learner	viii
Pacing lessons builds Memory	ix
Mental Processing in Reading	ix
Who can teach Professsor Bloomer's Reading Program	x
Assess yourself as a teacher	x
Who can learn from Professor Bloomer's reading program	x
Teaching Professor Bloomers Reading Program	x

Professor Bloomer's No-Nonsense Lessons

LESSON CONTENTS

				Teacher's Pages	Student's Pages
Lesson 1	Letter/Sound	/A/	as in FAT	1	1
Lesson 2	Letter/Sound	/T/	as in TAP	8	3
Lesson 3	Letter/Sound	/S/	as in SAT	15	5
Lesson 4	Letter/Sound	/M/	as in MAT	20	8
Lesson 5	Letter/Sound	/R/	as in RAN	26	12
Lesson 6	Letter/Sound	/G/	as in GOOD	31	16
Lesson 7	Letter/Sound	/F/	as in FAT	36	20
Lesson 8	Letter/Sound	/W/	as in WET	44	26
Lesson 9	Letter/Sound	/D/	as in DOG	55	34
Lesson 10	Letter/Sound	/N/	as in NUT	66	42
Lesson 11	Letter/Sound	/U/	as in NUT	75	50
Lesson 12	Letter/Sound	/H/	as in HAT	85	58
Lesson 13	Letter/Sound	/J/	as in JET	94	66
Lesson 14	Letter/Sound	/L/	as in LIKE	103	74
Lesson 15	Letter/Sound	/C/	as in CUT	112	83
Lesson 16	Letter/Sound	/I/	as in INSIST	121	91
Lesson 17	Letter/Sound	/V/	as in VEST	131	99
Lesson 18	Letter/Sound	/K/	as in KICK	140	107
Lesson 19	Letter/Sound	/B/	as in BAD	150	115
Lesson 20	Letter/Sound	/O/	as in TOP	160	123
Lesson 21	Letter/Sound	/Y/	as in YET	170	131
Lesson 22	Letter/Sound	/P/	as in POT	180	139
Lesson 23	Letter/Sound	/E/	as in NET	190	147
Lesson 24	Letter/Sound	/Z/	as in ZOO	210	155
Lesson 25	Letter/Sound	/X/	as in TAX	211	163
A Short History:				222	---

Professor Bloomer's No-Nonsense Reading Program
Lesson 1

Lesson 1 The letter/sound /A/ and the capital letter 'A'

This lesson introduces the letter/sound /A/ paired with the capital letter 'A.'

Letter/sound: /A/ as in TAP

Letter form: **A**

The capital letter 'A' is formed with three lines, moving from top to bottom and left to right.
1. The first stroke starts at the top of the letter/sound and slants down to the left.
2. The second stroke starts in the same place as the first stroke but slants down to the right.
3. The third stroke is a horizontal line that connects the middles of the first two lines.

Word: A

1. Introduce the letter/sound /A/ (Student workbook page 1)
Teacher: Today you are going to learn how to read a letter and its sound. I will write the letter on the board or on a separate piece of paper and you look at it carefully.

[Teacher writes the letter/sound /A/, describing and showing the strokes as she writes.]

Teacher: This letter sounds like /A/, /A/, /A/. Can you say that sound?

Learner: /A/, /A/, /A/.

Teacher: Good. Open your workbook

to the page for the letter/sound /A/ On this page, can you find the Letter that is like the one I wrote?

Please trace the letter/sound with your finger, and call it /A/, /A/, /A/.

[Learner traces the letter/sound and says /A/, /A/, /A/.]

Teacher: Look how I write /A/ /A/ is like the top of a house with a bar across it. Now, you write /A/ in your book. You can write it on the line next to the 'A' printed there.

[Learner writes 'A' in his book.]

[Teacher looks at written 'A.']

Teacher: That's Good. (Or point out any good features and ask learner to do another one

. Please pronounce what you have written in your book. Say it three times.

Learner: /A/, /A/, /A/.

Teacher: Now write /A/ again. Say /A/ as you write it.

Learner writes /A/ on his paper, saying /A/ softly as he writes.

Teacher points to letter/sound /A/ on page: Pronounce this letter/sound three times.

Learner: /A/, /A/, /A/.

You may want to repeat this part of each lesson several times on separate days to help with the writing skill and build the letter/sound correspondence.

Professor Bloomer's No-Nonsense Reading Program
Lesson 1

A

PICTURES TO LABEL

A

A

A

Professor Bloomer's No-Nonsense Reading Program
Lesson 1

Use the Letter/sound
Teacher: /A/ is really a word that you have just learned to read and write. Do you know what it means?
Learner: /A/ thing. One thing

2. Pictures to label (Student workbook page 1)
Teacher emphasizes that /A/ means one and only one thing.]
Teacher: Look below on your page. Can you find a picture of /A/ fox? Can you find some foxes? What is the difference between these pictures?

Learner: There are two foxes in this picture, and a single fox in that picture:

Teacher: Can you write the word /A/ under /A/ fox? Can you say it as you write it]
otice that the label helps you know what is in the picture.

[Learner writes 'A' under the picture and pronounces /A/ as in f**at**
[Teacher checks to see whether the learner has labeled the correct picture.]

Teacher: Can you find some other pictures to label /A/?

Learner: There is /A/ camel and /A/ pig.

Teacher: Can you label them with the Letter/sound /A/ and say what you are writing?

[Learner labels the other pictures and pronounces /A/ softly.]

[Throughout the day, teacher points out a desk, a book, a pencil, a piece of paper, and other items, so the learner becomes familiar with this Letter/sound and word.]
From time to time the teacher can call some learners to the board to write and sound the Letter/sound /A/. Pictures can be used to illustrate the concept.

Comments
Be sure that the learner understands that /A/ represents a single item. Avoid pointing out nouns that begin with a vowel and call for "an" instead of /A/ (as in "an animal").

Spend as much time as the learner needs on this and all other lessons. If necessary, find other pictures of single objects for practice reading and writing and saying /A/. The learner should know this Letter/sound thoroughly before you move on. Do not hurry.

Review to begin in the next day's session

**Pictures to label (continued)
(Students Workbook page 2)**

Teacher: In the last lesson, you began to learn to read. You learned one Letter/sound that is also a word. Do you remember what it was?

Learner: /A/.

Teacher: That's right. Can you write /A/?

[Learner writes /A/ and says /A/. Learner continues to write the Letter/sound and say it several times.]

(Students Workbook Page 2)

Teacher: Can you write /A/ under the correct picture that shows only one thing and say /A/

Teacher: Do you remember what /A/ means?

Learner: It means one.

Teacher: Good! Now look at the next page in your workbook. There are some pictures. Can you find a dog, a frog, a cat, a rabbit?|

Professor Bloomer's No-Nonsense Reading Program
Lesson 1

A

A

A

A

A

Lesson 2   The Letter/sound /T/ and the capital Letter 'T'

This lesson introduces the Letter/sound /T/ paired with the capital Letter/sound 'T.' It also begins to teach the concept of using elements to build words and of putting sounds together. It shows the relationship of writing, speaking, and reading.

Notes to teacher:
This lesson should take at least two sessions or more, each preferably separated by a whole day. This separation builds the memory processes. Judge by the quality of the learner's responses when to stop a session.

Allowing the learner to rest between sessions provides time for the learning to become solidified.

1. Letter/sound: /T/ as in TOP. The sound /T/ is formed by stopping a column of air with the tongue pressed against the roof of the mouth just behind the upper front teeth and then releasing. The release is not accompanied by vibration of the vocal cords. /T/ is unvoiced, a voiced /T/ sounds /D/.

Letter form::   T he capital Letter/sound 'T' is formed with two lines.

1. The first stroke is a horizontal line drawn from left to right, at the top of the Letter/sound.
2. The second stroke is a vertical line from the middle of the first stroke to the bottom of the Letter/sound.

Words: AT, TAT

Session 1

Review the previous lesson Procedure, Teacher's Manual page 6, (Use separate Lined paper **/A/**

   Since we are going to use our previous letter sounds in our new lesson to make words. In each lesson we will do a review to refresh our learners memory. This process not only enhances the learner's memory, but also may alert teachers to areas which need additional work.

   There are two possible procedures for this exercise.

Professor Bloomer's No-Nonsense Reading Program
Lesson 2
Review the previous lesson /(continued)

Review Procedure **A**: (Copy and Say)
A. Copy and say is the procedure for learners who are having difficulty
The teacher writes and says each letter/sound and word, one letter/sound at a time. The learner learner copies and says each letter sound

Review procedure **B**: (Dictation)
B. Dictation is the standard review procedure. Letter/sounds and words are presented as spelling words. The teacher pronounces each word, uses it in a sentence, and then pronounces the word again. The student writes it

Introduce the new Letter/sound /T/, Procedure: Teacher's Manual page 1; **(Student workbook page 3)**

Teacher: That's fine. Now you remember /A/ very well. You are ready to learn another Letter/sound now.
Teacher: Open your book to the page for /T./ Please trace the Letter/sound with your finger, and call it /T/ /T./ Now I will write the Letter/sound /T/' You watch and see how I make it. It looks like a telephone pole, doesn't it

Teacher writes the Letter/sound /T/ on the board , explaining how it is made.]
Teacher: This Letter/sound is pronounced /T/, /T/, /T/. Now you say it.

Learner: /T/, /T/, /T/.

? Now, you make a /T/ in your book, next to the one that is printed there. Again and say the Letter/sound strokes Letter/sound formation as you make it.

[Learner writes the Letter/sound /T/ on his paper and says /T/.]

Teacher points to Letter/sound /T/ on page: Now, what does this Letter/sound sound like? Please say it three times.

Learner: /T/, /T/, /T/.

[If learner pronounces incorrectly, teacher corrects softly.]

Teacher: Now, please write /T/ on your paper, and pronounce it as you write it.

[Learner writes /T/. and says /T/ softly as he writes.]

Professor Bloomer's No-Nonsense Reading Program
Lesson 2

Introduce the new Letter/sound (continued)

Teacher points to Letter/sound /A/:
Look at this Letter/sound. on the board . It sounds like /A/. Now you say it three times.

Learner: /A/, /A/, /A/.

Teacher: That's fine. You remembered.

Teacher points to the /T/: Now please pronounce this Letter/sound three times.

Learner: /T/, /T/, /T/.

Teacher: Let's make a game. I will call on one girl who will say /A/. or /T/ and I will call on a boy and he will come up to the board and point to which Letter/sound the girl has sounded. Then we will turn it around. (Let all the learners participate in the game.) My, you are all doing well.

Constructive Synthesis Phonetics, Procedure, Teacher's Manual page 8, (use separate lined paper)

Putting Letter/sounds and sounds together is the most important process in independent reading. It allows beginning readers to convert the Letter/sounds they see into the words they hear. It enables the learner to figure out new words and is essential for reading independence. The learner who fails to master this process can only memorize individual words. Teach your learner to use this procedure left to right for all new words

You may find it useful to illustrate this process with a word for an old-fashioned form of lace: 'TAT.' First, show the Letter/sounds widely separated.

T...................A.....................T

Then show the Letter/sounds closer together.
T............A............T

Finally, show the Letter/sounds right next to each other.

AT   T

Teach the word 'TAT' using the same method of combining sounds and Letter/sounds as above. Have the learner practice it a few times and then label the picture.

T

PICTURES TO LABEL

AT

AT

AT

TAT

Some learners catch on quickly and can then figure out new words. They are limited only by their memory capacity and the Letter/sounds they know. Other learners, particularly those who have failed with other methods, may require considerable practice. They may need help putting together each new word for several lessons. Be patient, and take the time necessary to ensure that the process becomes automatic.

Pictures to label Procedure, Teacher's Manual page 10, **(Student workbook page 3 & 4)**
Teacher: That's fine. Now can you find the picture of the girl is at the chalk board? Can you write the word 'AT' under the picture where the boy is at the door?

[Learner writes the word 'AT.']

Can you find the picture in which the children are <u>not</u> at the door? What will we write jhere?

Learner: Nothing

Teacher checks and continues: Now find and label the picture where the Wolf at the door.

[Learner writes and teacher checks.]

Teacher Now find the picture of the lady sitting?. Can you see she has something in her hands? That lady is tatting. It is a kind of knitting people used to make lace for clothes. Can you write the word TAT beneath her picture?

Learner writes the word TAT sounding the Letter/sounds as he writes

Teacher: That's fine. Now, please write the word two more times and sound it as you do, so you will be sure to remember it.

[Learner writes across the top of the page.]

Teacher: Very good. Study and pronounce this word at home. Tomorrow we will see who remembers these new letter/sounds that make a whole word. And we will see if we remember how to write them, too.

Professor Bloomer's No-Nonsense Reading Program
Lesson 2

AT

AT

AT

TAT

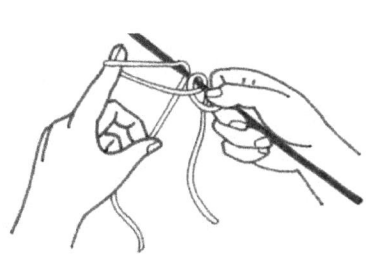
TAT

A	AT	TAT	**A**
AT	TAT	**AT**	A
TAT	**TAT**	A	AT

13

Professor Bloomer's No-Nonsense Reading Program
Lesson 2

Session 2

Review the previous session
Begin by having the learner write and pronounce /A/ and /T/ several times. Then have the learner practice saying and writing the words 'AT' and 'TAT.'

5. Finding Word Pairs and Reading Aloud Procedure, Teacher's Manual page 12, **(Student workbook page 4)**

Directions: This exercise gives the learner practice in distinguishing among words he sees and in making selections in multiple-choice questions.
Teacher: In each row, two words are exactly the same. Find these two words, circle them, and say them out loud. then read the whole line out loud.

FIND THE WORD AND READ ALOUD

A	AT	TAT	A
AT	TAT	AT	A
TAT	TAT	A	AT

Professor Bloomer's No-Nonsense Reading Program
Lesson 3

Lesson 3   The Letter/sound /S/

Lesson 3 introduces the Letter/sound /S/ and its combinations with the preceding Letter/sounds, serving to expand the notion of synthesizing words from the phonemic elements.

Timing Note: This lesson should take at least TWO or more sessions preferably separated by a whole day. Teachers should judge by the quality of the learner's responses whether to continue on or to rehearse for a longer period. Resting time between learning sessions for consolidation of learning is essential. Remember to start each session with a Review. Time is not important, Quality is.

Letter/sound: /S/, as in SOME. /S/ is formed by nearly closing the mouth with the tongue just behind the upper front teeth and a column of air is forced out. The vocal chords do not vibrate when SSS is sounded. A voiced /S/ sounds /Z/. /S/ sounds like air going out of a tire.

Letter/sound formation: **S**

'S' The capital Letter/sound 'S' is made from two curved lines

> 1. The first line begins at two o'clock and curves counterclockwise to the left, to the middle of the Letter/sound.
>
> 2. The second line continues from the first, circling clockwise to the bottom and ending at eight o'clock

Words: SAT, AS.

1. Beginning Review: Procedure, Teachers manual Page 6-7: **/A/, /T/, AT, TAT**
Yesterday we learned to read two Letter/sounds and two words. Who remembers the Letter/sounds?

Learner: /A/ and /T/

Teacher: "That's fine", writes the word AT on the board. There are two Letter/sounds in the word. What are the two Letter/sounds?

Learner: /A/ and /T/.

Teacher: Let's sound these Letter/sounds. (Teacher points to the Letter/sounds as the learners sound them.)

Learner: /A/—/T/, AT;   /A/—/T/, AT;   /T/-/A/—/T/. TAT   /T/-/A/-/T/, TAT

Teacher: Asks individuals to say the Letter/sound as she points to them. Teacher reviews thoroughly.

2 Introducing the Letter/sound: /S/, Procedure: Teacher's Manual page 1; **(Student workbook page 5)**

Now, today we will learn another Letter/sound. This Letter/sound is /S/ and it sounds like your mother's tea kettle /S/—/S/. You make an S like a long curly snake. Teacher writes S and says, I'll put a line under it so we'll know what it is. Let's all say /S/ together. (Learners say /S/ /S/ /S/.) Open your books to this page. Draw a /S/ in your books. (continue as in Units I and II, until learners are completely acquainted with the new Letter/sound.) What were our old Letter/sounds again?

Learner: /A/ /T/.

Teacher: (Writes AT on the board.) What word did we have when we put those two sounds together?

Learner: /AT/.

Teacher: Let's put those together with our new Letter/sound (Writes SAT on the board.) How many Letter/sounds do we know now?
Learner: We know three Letter/sounds.

3. Constructive Synthesis: Procedure: Teacher's Manual page 8; (on separate lined paper)
Teacher: Let's pronounce each Letter/sound as I point to it.
Learner: /S/ /A/ /T/ /SAT/. (They keep saying these sounds faster and faster until someone recognizes that they make a word. Learners say the word then over a few times together, then each one by one.)

Teacher: Write the word SAT in your books. Pronounce the word. (Teacher drills them with the game, or a similar one, as of the day before. Take the word apart and join it again. She may walk across the room and sit on a chair, asking the learners to watch her. After walking back to position, she asks them what she did.)

Learner: Sat on the chair. (Some may not fully comprehend. The teacher praises any correct answers.)

Teacher: And SAT is a new word which we have put together with what Letter/sounds?
Learner: /S/ /A/ /T/

Teacher: That's fine. We are learning to make new words, and to read.
Use the same procedure for the word "AS"

Note: Each of the words should be written at least twice by each learner in addition to the labeling.

4. Pictures to LABEL: Procedure Teacher's Manual page 10: **(Student workbook page 5)**
Have the learners identify meaning pictures and label the proper ones with SAT as before.

S _____

_____

PICTURES TO NAME

SAT

SAT

FIND THE LETTER

S	AT	**S**AT
T	SA**T**	AS
S	A	A**S**
T	A	SA**T**
S	**S**AT	A

Professor Bloomer's No-Nonsense Reading Program
Lesson 3

Find the Letter and read aloud: Procedure, Teacher's Manual page 12: **(Student workbook page 5)**

S	AT	**S**AT
T	SA**T**	AS
S	A	A**S**
T	A	SA**T**
S	**S**AT	A

The following exercises may to be used for paced review later in the day or following Letter/sound and word review on the next teaching day.

MATCHING EXERCISE, Procedure, Teacher's Manual page 16, **(Student workbook page 6) Directions:** The learner is to draw a line from the words in the first colimn to that same word in the second column.

```
SAT         TAT
A           AT
AT          AS
TAT         SAT
AS          A
```

FIND THE WORD AND READ ALOUD, Procedure, Teacher's Manual page 16, **(Student workbook page 6)**

A	TAT	SAT	**A**
AS	AT	**AS**	SAT
AT	SAT	**AT**	TAT
TAT	**TAT**	AS	SAT
SAT	AT	**SAT**	TAT

DICTATION, Procedure, Teacher's Manual page 16, **(Student workbook page 6)** **(use separate lined paper, if necessary)**

/T/, /S/ /A/, AT, SAT, AS, TAT.

PICTURES TO LABEL: Procedure, Teacher's Manual page 10: **(Student workbook page 7)** having the learners identify the pictures of SAT and label them.

18

PICTURE PHRASES

SAT

SAT

SAT

SAT

Professor Bloomer's No-Nonsense Reading Program
Lesson 4

Lesson 4 THE Letter/sound /M/

Purpose: Lesson 4 introduces the Letter/sound /M/ as in MAT. It is designed as a continuation of lessons I, II and III. Here the learners expand their concept of synthesizing words, and increase the number of Letter/sounds with which they can work. Learners begin to expand their meaning vocabularies by using some of the new words.

Timing Note: This lesson should take at least THREE sessions preferably separated by a whole day. Teachers should judge by the quality of the learner's responses whether to continue on or to rehearse for a longer period. Resting time between learning sessions for consolidation of learning is essential. Remember to start each session with a Review. Time is not important, Quality is.

Letter/sound /M/: as in mad /M/ made by closing the mouth with the lips and forcing a column of air through the nose. This is accompanied by the vibration of the vocal chords.

Letter formation: **M**

'M' The capital Letter/sound 'M' is made from four lines

1. The first stroke is a vertical line from the top to the bottom of the letter. This line may slant slightly to the left
2. The second stroke starts at the top of the letter and angles down to the right to the bottom of the letter at about 60 degrees
3. The third stroke starts to the right of the first stroke at the top of the letter and angles down to the left at about 60 degrees to meet with the second stroke at the bottom of the letter.
4. The fourth stroke starts at the top of the third stroke. It is a vertical line from the top to the bottom of the lettet. This line may slant slightly to the right

Words: SAM, MAT, TAM, MAST, MAMA, MAM, AM

Beginning Review: Procedure, Teachers manual Page 6-7: **(Use separate lined paper for this exercise)**
　　　Letter/sounds **/A/ /T/ and /S/** and the words **AT, TAT, SAT, AS**

Introducing the Letter/sound: /M/, Procedure: Teacher's Manual page 1; **(Student workbook page 8)**
　　　The Letter/sound /M/as in MAT

Professor Bloomer's No-Nonsense Reading Program
Lesson 4

M

PICTURES TO NAME

SAM

TAM

MAMA

MAST

Professor Bloomer's No-Nonsense Reading Program
Lesson 4

FIND THE LETTER

M	AT	SA**M**	SAT
S	MAT	TAT	MA**S**T
M	**M**A**M**A	AT	**M**AST
T	SAM	MAS**T**	MAMA
M	SAT	AS	**M**AST

MATCH AND LABEL

SAM SAT
MAMA
MAT
TAM
MAST

TAM

MAMA   SAM SAT

MAT

MAST

Professor Bloomer's No-Nonsense Reading Program
Lesson 4

Constructive Synthesis: Procedure: Teacher's Manual page 8; **(Use separate lined paper for this exercise)**

    SAM, MAT, TAM, MAMA, MAST

Pictures to Label: Procedure Teacher's Manual page 10: **(Student workbook page 8)**

    SAM, TAM, MAMA, MAST

Find the Letter/sound: and read aloud Procedure Teachers Manual page 12 **(Student Workbook page 9).** for learner independence

Find the Letter/sound **/M/, /S/, /M/, /T/, /M/.**

M	AT	SA**M**
S	MAT	MA**S**T
M	**MAMA**	TAT
T	SAM	MA**T**
M	SAT	**M**AST

Match and Label: Procedure, Teacher's Manual page 21: **(Student Workbook page 9)** The learner is to identify the picture that goes with each word and draw a line from the word to the picture. He is then to label the picture. The teacher will continue to help learners as needed, but allowing the child to print the label themselves.

Matching words: Procedure, Teacher's Manual page 16: **(Student Workbook page 10)**

AM	MAST
MAMA	MAT
MAT	MAM
MAST	MAMA
TAM	AM
MAM	TAM

Finding word pairs and Reading aloud: Procedure, Teacher's Manual page 16: (**Student Workbook page 10**).

AM	MAMA	SAM	**AM**
SAM	**SAM**	TAM	SAT
MAST	TAM	**MAST**	TAT
MAMA	MAT	SAT	**MAMA**
TAM	SAM	**TAM**	TAT

Dictation: Procedure, Teacher's Manual page 16: (Student Workbook page 10) **(Use separate lined paper for this exercise)**

/A/, /T/, /S/, /M/, AM, SAM, MAST, MAMA, TAM, SAM, SAT,

Pictures Phrases: Procedure, Teacher's Manual Page 21,**(Student workbook page 11)**

Find the picture of Sam sitting on the next page. Can we write Sam under that picture? Can you find some pictures of boat masts? Point to the picture of the boat and the mast. Can we write the word Mast under it?
Find the picture of Sam and the Mast. What is Sam doing? Can we write Sam sat a Mast? Help the learners label the rest of the pictures on the page. Use same procedure for other picture phrases.

Professor Bloomer's No-Nonsense Reading Program
Lesson 4

PICTURE PHRASES

SAM SAT

MAST

TAM

SAM SAT

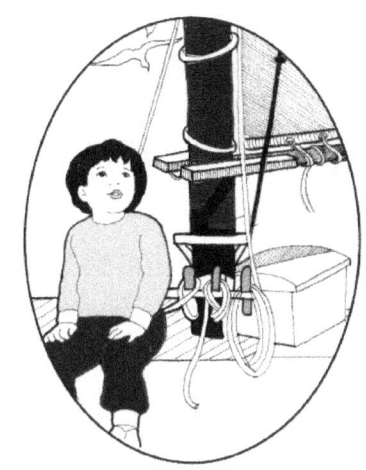

SAM SAT AT A MAST

MAMA

Professor Bloomer's No-Nonsense Reading Program
Lesson 5

Lesson 5 THE Letter/sound /R/

Purpose: Lesson 5 introduces the Letter/sound /R/ as in RAN the lesson increases the words the learner is able to synthesize and the sentences and phrase he is able to read and spell.

Timing Note: This lesson should take at least THREE sessions preferably separated by s whole day the. Teachers should judge by the quality of the learner's responses whether to continue on or to rehearse for a longer period. Resting time between learning sessions for consolidation of learning is essential. Remember to start each session with a Review. Time is not important, Quality is.

Letter/sound: /R/. /R/ is formed by nearly closing the mouth with the tongue far back against the roof of the mouth. A column of air is forced out between the tip of the tongue and the roof of the mouth. This is accompanied by a vibration of the vocal chords. /R/ is the sound a rooster makes when crowing.

Letter/sound Formation: **R**
'R' The capital Letter/sound 'R' is made from three lines

>   1. The first stroke is a straight vertical line from the top of the Letter to the bottom.
>
>   2. The second stroke is a horizontal 'u' shape that begins at the top of the first line and proceeds out to the right returning to connect at the middle of the vertical line.
>
>   3. The third stroke begins the connection in the middle of the vertical line and proceeds downward and to the right at 45 degrees.

Words: ART, RAM, TAR, RAT, STAR, START, TART, MAR, TRAM, ARM.

Beginning Review: Procedure, Teachers manual Page 6-7: **(Use separate lined paper for this exercise)**
>   Letter/sounds **/A/, /T/, /M/, and /S/, and the words AT, TAT, SAT, AS, MAT, MAMA, SAM, TAM, MAST.**

Introducing the Letter/sound: /R/ , Procedure: Teacher's Manual page 1;**(Student Workbook page 12)**
>   The Letter/sound /R/ as in RAT

Constructive Synthesis: Procedure: Teacher's Manual page 8; **(Use separate lined paper for this exercise)**
>   **RAM, RAT, TAR, STAR, TART, TRAM, ARM, ART,**

Professor Bloomer's No-Nonsense Reading Program
Lesson 5

R

PICTURES TO NAME

STAR

RAM

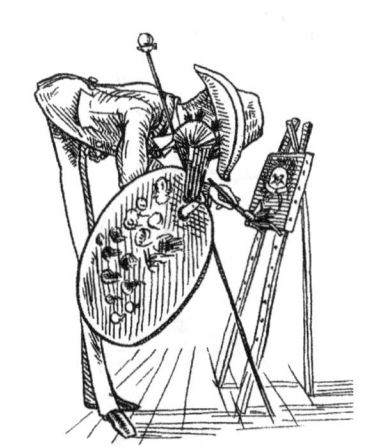
ART

RAT

TRAM

MATCH AND LABEL

TRAM
TAM
RAM
STAR
MAST
RAT
ART
TART

STAR

RAT

ART

TAM

RAM

TART

TRAM

MAST

TRAM

FIND THE LETTER AND READ ALOUD

R	MAT	**R**AT	SAT
S	TAR	RAM	**S**TAR
T	**T**AM	SAM	RA**T**
R	MAMA	TA**R**	MAM
M	RA**M**	START	TART
R	SAM	AM	**R**AM

Professor Bloomer's No-Nonsense Reading Program
Lesson 5

Pictures to NAME: Procedure Teacher's Manual page 10: **(Student Workbook page 12)** STAR, RAM, ART, RAT, TRAM

Match and Label: Procedure, Teacher's Manual page 21: **(Student Workbook page 13)**

Find the Letter and reading aloud: Procedure, Teacher's Manual page 12: **(Student Workbook page 13)**
Follow the procedure from lesson 3.

R	MAT	**R**AT
S	**S**TAR	RAM
T	RAM	RA**T**
R	MAMA	TA**R**
M	RA**M**	START
R	T**R**AM	AM

Matching words: Procedure, Teacher's Manual page 16: **(Student Workbook page 14)**.

RAT	RAM
STAR	START
TAR	RAT
RAM	TRAM
START	TAR
TRAM	STAR

Finding word pairs and Reading aloud: Procedure, Teacher's Manual page 16: **(Student Workbook page 14)**

STAR	RAT	**RAM**	**RAM**
RAT	START	**RAT**	ART
TRAM	**TAR**	RAT	**TAR**
STAR	**STAR**	START	RAT
ART	STAR	TRAM	**ART**

Dictation: Procedure, Teacher's Manual page 16: **(Student Workbook page 14)** (Use separate lined paper for this exercise)
/A/, /T/, /S/, /M/, /R/, RAM, STAR, RAT, TART. MAST, ART, ARM, START

Picture Phrases Procedure, Teacher's Manual Page 21, **((Student Workbook page 15)**   MAMA , RAM, SAM SAT AT A MAST., TAM, TART(S), MAMA

Professor Bloomer's No-Nonsense Reading Program
Lesson 5

PICTURE PHRASES

MAMA

RAM

ARM

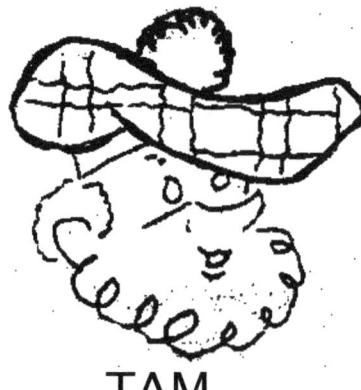
TAM

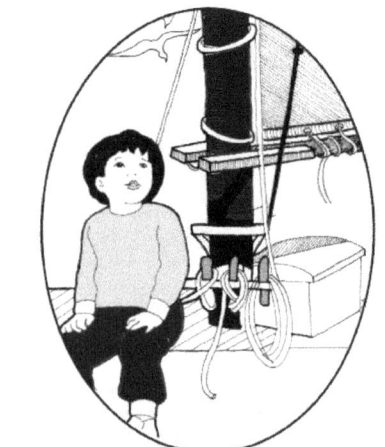
SAM SAT AT A MAST

SAM SAT

TARTS

MAMA

Professor Bloomer's No-Nonsense Reading Program
Lesson 6

Lesson 6 THE Letter/sound /G/

Purpose; Lesson 6 introduces the Letter/sound /G/ as in good and related words, and builds new word concepts. The concepts of how language is formed is stressed.

Timing Note: This lesson should take at least THREE sessions preferably separated by a whole day. Teachers should judge by the quality of the learner's responses whether to continue on or to rehearse for a longer period. Resting time between learning sessions for consolidation of learning is essential. Remember to start each session with a Review Time is not important, Quality is.

Letter/sound: /G/, as in Good. /G/ is formed by stopping a column of air by pressing the middle of the tongue against the roof of the mouth and then releasing it. The release is accompanied by a vibration of the vocal chords. /G/ which is not voiced sounds /K/

.Letter Formation: G

'G' The capital letter 'G' is made from two strokes one curved and one straight.

    1. The first stroke starts at 2 o'clock and curves to the left in a circular path around to three o'clock

    2. The second short horizontal stroke starts at three o'clock and proceeds to the left less than half way to the curved line

Words: GAS, GRASS, RAG, SAG, TAG, STAG, GRAMA.

Beginning Review: Procedure, Teachers manual Page 6-7: **(Use separate lined paper for this exercise)**

    Letter/sounds **/A/, /T/, /S/, /M/, /R/,**
    **Words: TAT, SAT, MAT, MAMA, TAM, MAST, RAM, STAR, RAT, START,
MAST,**   **ART, ARM.**

Introducing the Letter/sound: /G/, Procedure: Teacher's Manual page 1; **(Student Workbook page 16)**
The Letter/sound /G/ as in grass

Professor Bloomer's No-Nonsense Reading Program
Lesson 6

G

PICTURES TO NAME

GRASS

TAG

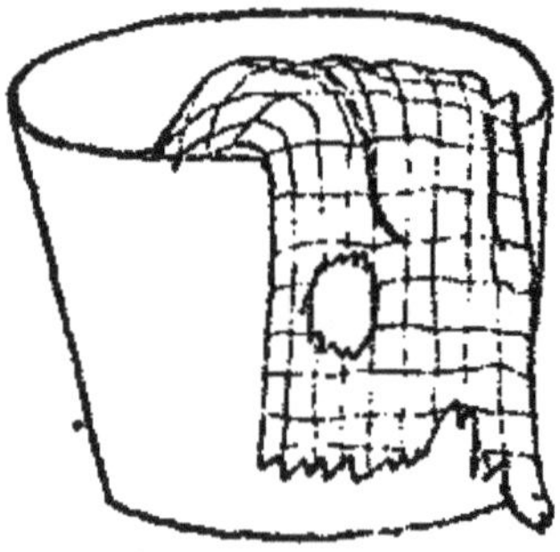

GRAM

RAG

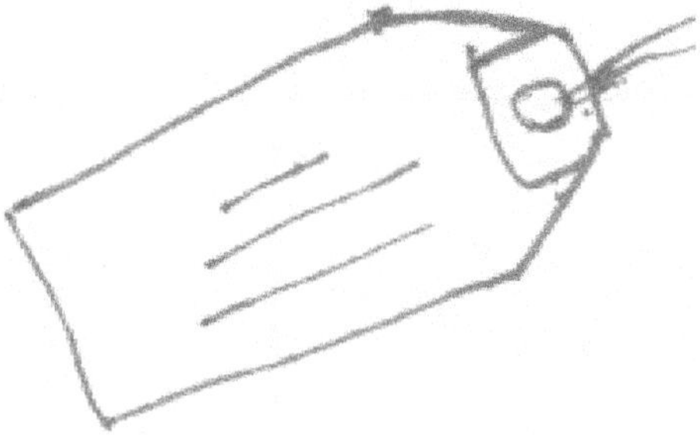

TAG

STAG

MATCH AND LABEL

GAS
TAG
STAR
TRAM
RAM
RAG
GRASS

 STAR

RAM

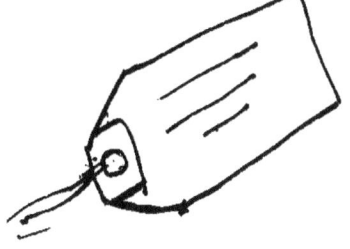
TAG

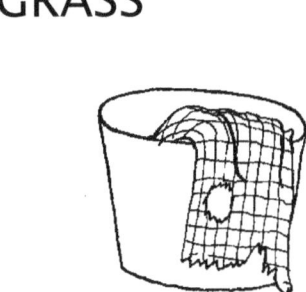
RAG

GRASS

GAS

TRAM

FIND THE LETTER

G	GAS	STAR	RAG
T	TAG	SAG	GAS
M	RAM	MAT	TAG
G	TRAM	GRASS	SAM
R	STAR	MAMA	TART
G	RAG	RAT	GRASS

Professor Bloomer's No-Nonsense Reading Program
Lesson 6

Constructive Synthesis: I Procedure: Teacher's Manual page 8; **(Use separate lined paper for this exercise)**

GAS, RAG, SAG, TAG, GRAMA, GRASS, STAG

Have the learners write the words as they sound them out left to right.

Pictures to Label: Procedure Teacher's Manual page 10: **(Student Workbook page 16)** GRASS, GRAMA, TAG, RAG, STAG, TAG.

Match and Label: Procedure, Teacher's Manual page 21: **(Student Workbook page 17)** Follow the procedure in lesson 3 is a meaning exercise. Some children may have more trouble than others. The teacher will continue to help learners as needed, but allowing the child to write the label themselves.

Find the Letter: Procedure, Teacher's Manual page 12: **(Student Workbook page 17)**

G	STAR	**G**AS
T	**TAG**	SAG
M	TAG	**M**AT
G	TRAM	**G**RASS
R	STA**R**	MAMA
G	**RAG**	RAT

Matching words: Procedure, Teacher's Manual page 16: **(Student Workbook page 18)**

GAS	RAG
SAG	GRASS
RAG	GAS
GRASS	GAG
GAG	TAG
TAG	SAG

Finding word pairs and Reading aloud: Procedure, Teacher's Manual page 16: **(Student Workbook page 18)**

RAG	**GRASS**	MAT	**GRASS**
RAG	SAG	**RAG**	TAG
GAS	TRAM	GRASS	**GAS**
SAG	**TAG**	GAS	**TAG**
TAG	GRAM	**SAG**	**SAG**
GAG	TAG	RAG	**GAG**

Professor Bloomer's No-Nonsense Reading Program
Lesson 6

Sounds in words: Procedure, Teacher's Manual page 32, **(Student Workbook page 18)** (A new exercise for lesson 6.) Sounds In Words is designed to strengthen phonemic skills and help the learner focus to sort for stimuli from a complex array. The teacher pronounces a Letter/sound for each row. The learner is to find the Letter/sound and read the all the word containing it. There may be more than word in the line. The sequence of Letter/sounds for lesson 6 is as follow /M/, /G/, /R/, /T/, /R/, /G/, /M/, /S/.

RATS	**TAM**	STAR
RAM	**GRASS**	TAGS
TARTS	GAS	MAST
SAG	**TRAM**	**MAST**
MAST	MAMA	**STAR**
TRAM	**TAGS**	RAT
RAGS	**RAM**	**TAM**
MAST	TAM	**SAT**

Dictation: Procedure, Teacher's Manual Page 16, **(Student Workbook page 19)** **(Use separate lined paper for this exercise)**

Dictation should be presented in several sessions limited to lists of eight to ten Letter/sounds and words presented in random order. If there are many errors in the dictation exercise, you are moving to fast, the lessons are too long, or you are not allowing incubation time ,or sufficient repetitions or pacing is too fast for the learning to solidify in memory.

A/, /T/, /S/, /M/, /R/, /G/, STAR, GAS, RAG, SAG, TAG, GRAMA, GRASS, STAG, START, RAT, TART MAST, ART, ARM, START .

How many words can you make? Procedure, Teacher's Manual page 32, **(Student Workbook page 19)**

A new exercise for lesson 6. It allows the learners to practice their synthesis skills. It has the advantage of increasing flexibility and provides the opportunity for learner creativity. Here capable learners may shine. But everyone should have some success

Directions- On this page are some Letter/sounds. Put them together to make as many words as you can. The Letter/sounds are **/G/, /T/, /R/, /S/, /A/, /M/.**

Professor Bloomer's No-Nonsense Reading Program
Lesson 7

Lesson 7 THE Letter/sound /F/

Purpose: Unit VII introduces the Letter/sound /F/ , AS IN FAT a new Letter/sound and increases the words. In addition it begins making and understanding words together in meaningful phrases.

Timing Note: This lesson should take at least THREE sessions preferably separated by a whole day. Teachers should judge by the quality of the learner's responses whether to continue on or to rehearse for a longer period. Resting time between learning sessions for consolidation of learning is essential. Remember to start each session with a Review. Time is not important, Quality is.

Letter/sound: /F/. /F/ is made by placing the upper front teeth close to the lower lip and blowing a column of air between. The vocal chords do not vibrate. A voiced /F/ sounds /V/.

Letter Formation: F

The capital Letter/sound 'F' is composed of three straight lines

    1. The first stroke is a vertical line from the top to the bottom of the Letter/sound.
    2. The second stroke is half the length of the first. It starts at the top of the verti cal line and proceeds perpendicular to the right.
    3. The third stroke is half the length of the first. It starts at the middle of the vertical line and proceeds perpendicular to the right.

Words: FAR, FARM, FAST, RAFT, AFT.

Sample phrases: FAT SAM, FAST SAM, A FAT RAT, A FAST RAT, A FAT RAT SAT, A FAST TRAM, FAT SAM SAT.

Beginning Review: Procedure, Teachers manual Page 6-7: **(Use separate lined paper for this exercise)**
    Letter/sounds **/A/, /T/, /S/, /M/, /R/, /G/**
    Words, TAT, SAT, MAT, MAMA, TAM, MAST RAM, STAR, RAT, START, MAST, ART, ARM, GAS, GRASS, RAG, SAG, TAG, STAG, GRAMA.

Introducing the Letter/sound /F/, Procedure: Teacher's Manual page 1; **(Student Workbook page 13)**/F/
The Letter/sound /F/ as in FAT

Constructive Synthesis: Procedure: Teacher's Manual page 8; **(Use separate lined paper for this exercise)**
    FAR, FARM, FAST, RAFT, AFT, GAS, TAG, GRAMA, GRASS

F

PICTURES TO NAME

FAR

FARM

FAT

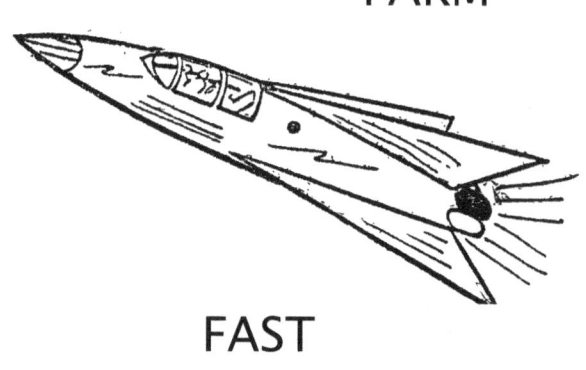
FAST

Professor Bloomer's No-Nonsense Reading Program
Lesson 7

Pictures to NAME: Procedure Teacher's Manual page 10: **(Student Workbook page 20)** FAR FARM FAT FAST

Match and Label: Procedure, Teacher's Manual page 21: **(Student Workbook page 21)**
\

Find the Letter/sound: Procedure, Teacher's Manual page 12: **(Student Workbook page 22)**

R	SAT	TAM	FA**R**M
T	FAR	S**T**AR	RAM
M	FAT	TRA**M**	SA**M**.
G	MAMA	SA**G**	RAFT
T	GAS	MA**T**	SA**T**
F	TART	**F**AR	RAG
M	RAT	**M**AT	SAT
T	GRASS	RAF**T**	MAS**T**

Matching Words and Finding Words Procedure, Teacher's Manual page 16: **(Student Workbook page 22)**

FAR	FAST
FAST	FAR
RAFT	GRASS
FARM	FAT
GRASS	Raft

Finding word pairs and Reading aloud: Procedure, Teacher's Manual page 16: **(Student Workbook page 22)**

FAST	**FAR**	FAT	**FAR**
FAST	FAR	**FAST**	GRAM
RAT	**RAT**	RAG	FAT
RAFT	MAT	MAST	**RAFT**
RAT	**FARM**	FAT	**FARM**
FAR	FARM	MAR	**FAR**

38

MATCH AND LABEL

FARM
FAST
TRAM
FAT
STAR
RAFT
GAS
TAM
RAT
FAR

Professor Bloomer's No-Nonsense Reading Program
Lesson 7

Sounds in words: Procedure, Teacher's Manual Page 32, **(Student Workbook page 23)**

The sequence to use in this lesson is as follow /S/, /T/, /R/, /M/, /S/, /F/, /G/, /M/.

   RAT**S**   TAM   FARM
   RAF**T**   GRASS   **T**AGS
   TA**R**TS   GAS   MAST
   SAG   TRA**M**S   FAST
   MA**S**TS   MAMA   FARM
   TRAMS   TAGS   RA**F**TS
   RA**G**S   RAMS   TAM
   FAST   TA**M**S   SAT

Dictation: Procedure, Teacher's Manual page 16: **(Student Workbook page 23) (Use separate lined paper for this exercise)**

 /A/, /T/, /S/, /M/, /R/, /G/, STAR, GAS, RAG, SAG, TAG, GRAMA, GRASS, STAG, START, RAT, TART, MAST, ART, ARM, START . I

How many words can you make? Procedure, Teacher's Manual Page 32 **(Student Workbook page 23)**
. The Letter/sounds are /T/, /S/, /M/, /A/, /F/, /G/. /R/

Phrases to Read Aloud and Write: Procedure, Teacher's Manual Page 37-38 **(Student Workbook page 24) (Use separate lined paper)**

Phrases and sentences are introduced in the following manner.
Teacher: Up to now, learners, we have been learning to read mostly words. We do not say things in just one word, but we say things in lots of words. If I say SAM, that is just a boy's name. It does not say anything about SAM. We can put other words with SAM and then we can tell more about him.

Let's take a word we know and put it with SAM and see what we get. (She writes the word SAM on the board, followed by SAT.)

Learner: SAM, SAT.
Teacher: Now, what does that tell us about SAM?

Learner: It says that SAM SAT.
Teacher: That's very good. (She writes the word FAT on the board.) Do we remember what this word is?

Learner: FAT.

Teacher: That's fine. Now, what's this? (Teacher writes the word SAM after the word FAT.
Learner: FAT SAM.

Teacher: What does this tell us about SAM?

Now look at the phrases on the page read each phrase

Class—He is FAT.
Teacher—That's wonderful, learners. (She adds the word SAT.) What does this tell us about SAM?
Class—SAM is FAT and he SAT.
Teacher—Fine. Now let's take some paper and write our sentence on it. Then we have a picture of the sentence. Can you find it and label it? (A similar procedure may be used with sentences such as A FAT RAT SAT or A FAST TRAM.)

Now look at the phrases on the page read each phrase say it and then write it on the line

Phrases to Read and Write (Use separate lined paper for this exercise)

```
FAT SAM_____
FAST SAM_____
A FAT RAT_____
A FAST RAT_____
A FAT RAM_____
SAM'S RAFT _____
A FAST RAFT _____
A FAST TRAM _____
FAT SAM SAT _____
A FAT RAT SAT _____
```

Completing Phrases: Procedure, Teacher's Manual Page 38–39, **(Student Workbook page 24)**

This is an exercise to train the learner to search for meaning from the printed word. This complex process is simplified for learning by the limited number pf Letter/sounds we have learned which allows us to focus the learner on this important process. The exercise is designed to increase learner independence and to use context clues to develop meaning. In many cases more than one Letter/sound can complete the word or words, but only one will be meaningful. The teacher should be sure the learners understand that the Letter/sound they are to fill in must add to the meaning in such a way as to make sense. Help those who have difficulty by showing them the number of possibilities and having them choose the right one. The first few of these exercises may be done by the class as a whole, discussing the various meanings from the possible words.

Teacher -- At the bottom of the page are some phrases. They each have a Letter/sound missing so they don't make sense. We need to find the missing Letter/sound so the phrase will make sense. Lets look at the first phrase. What Letter/sound would make sense? Could we use /M/? what word would that make?

Class- MAST

T- A MAST RAT does that make sense?

C- No

How about /T/ or /G/ do they make any sense?

C– No

T– what other Letter/sound might fit to make sense?

Class- /F/

T– That's right A FAST RAT. Continue the process for the remaining completion phrases. As the process is learned the children should develop more independence and ve able to perform this task with little assistance

Completing Phrases
    A __AST RAT.
    SAM'S __AFT
    A __AT RAM

Pictures Phrases: Procedure, Teacher's Manual Page 21, **(Student Workbook page 25)**

MAST, (SAM SAT AT A MAST). RAM, TAM FAR, STAR RAFT MAMA, FAST FARM FAT, RAT.

Professor Bloomer's No-Nonsense Reading Program
Lesson 7

SAM SAT AT A MAST

RAM

TAM

FAR

STAR

MAMA

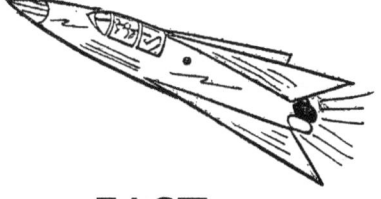
FAST

FARM

RAFT

FAT

RAT

LESSON 8 THE Letter/sound /W/

Purpose. Unit VIII introduces the Letter/sound /W/ and related words. The sound W is the first letter/sound which will require a special review to differentiate it from the Letter M. Learners increase their experiences with meaning and with sentences.

Timing Note: This lesson should take at least THREE sessions preferably separated by a whole day. Teachers should judge by the quality of the learner's responses whether to continue on or to rehearse for a longer period. Resting time between learning sessions for consolidation of learning is essential. Remember to start each session with a Review. Time is not important, Quality is.

Sound /W/. /W/ is formed by rounding the lips and forcing a column of air through, then slacking the lips to complete the sound. This is accompanied by a vibration of the vocal chords.

Letter formation W

'W' The capital letter 'W' is made with four straight lines.

> 1. The first stroke starts at the top of the letter and angles down to the right at about 60 degrees.

> 2. The second stroke starts at the top of the letter, a little less than a letter width to the right and angles down to the left at about 60 degrees to meet the first stroke at the bottom of the letter.

> 3. The third stroke starts at the top of the letter with the second stroke and angles down to the right at about 60 degrees

> 4. The fourth stroke starts at the top of the letter a little less than a letters width to the right and angles down to the left at about 60 degrees to meet the third stroke at the bot tom of the letter.

Words. SAW, WAS, RAW, SWAM, WAR, WARD, DRAW, WARM, STRAW, WAG, WART.

Phrases. A RAT WAS FAST. A RAT WAS FAT. DRAW A RAT. A RAT SAW A STAR. A RAT SWAM.

Professor Bloomer's No-Nonsense Reading Program
Lesson 8

Beginning Review Procedure, Teachers manual Page 6-7: **(Use separate lined paper for this exercise)**
sounds: /A/ /T/ /S/. /M/ /R/, /F/
words: FAR, FARM, FAST, RAFT, AFT, MAT, MAMA, MAST STAR, RAT START, GAS, GRASS, RAG, SAG, TAG, STAG, GRAMA

Introducing the sound /W/, Procedure: Teacher's Manual page 1; **(Student Workbook page 26)**
The Letter/Sound /W/, as in WAS

Constructive Synthesis: Procedure: Teacher's Manual page 8; for the words **(Use separate lined paper for this exercise)**

SAW, WAS, RAW, SWAM, WAR, WARD, DRAW, WARM, STRAW, WAG, WART.

Pictures to Label Procedure Teacher's Manual page 10: **(Student Workbook page 26)**
SAW, WAG, SAW, WAR, SWAM, WARM.

Match and Label Procedure, Teacher's Manual page 12: **(Student Workbook page 27**

SWAM, GRASS, RAFT, SAW, WARM, WAG, TAG, WAR.

Professor Bloomer's No-Nonsense Reading Program
Lesson 8

W _____

_____

PICTURES TO LABEL

SAW

SAW

WAG

WAR

SWAM

WARM

MATCH AND LABEL

SWAM
GRASS
RAFT
SAW
WARM
WAG
TAG
WAR

WARM

SWAM

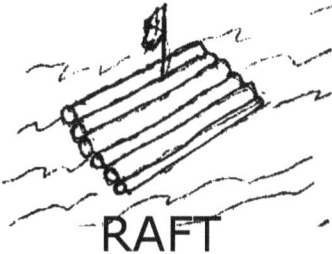
RAFT

SAW

TAG

GRASS

WAR

WAG

Professor Bloomer's No-Nonsense Reading Program
Lesson 8

Find the Letter. Procedure, Teacher's Manual Page 12, **(Student Workbook page 28)**

W	S**W**AM	SAT	TRAM
F	RA**F**T	SAW	**F**AR
R	GAS	FAT	G**R**ASS
G	TAR	TA**G**S	SAW
W	SAD	RAFT	**W**AR
S	TART	**S**AW	FARM
W	**W**ARM	STAR	FAST
G	FAT	WA**G**	**G**AS

Matching words Procedure, Teacher's Manual page 16: **(Student Workbook page 28)**

STRAW	WARM
SAW	WAG
STAR	FARM
WAG	STRAW
RAW	SAW
WAS	RAW
FARM	STAR
WARM	WAS

Finding word pairs and Reading aloud Procedure, Teacher's Manual page 16: **(Student Workbook page 28)**

SAW	MAT	FAR	**SAW**
RAW	WAR	**RAW**	WARM
WAS	**WAS**	SAM	SAW
WARM	**WAG**	RAG	**WAG**
WAS	WARM	**STRAW**	**STRAW**
WAR	WAS	SAW	**WAR**
SWAM	**WARM**	**WARM**	FARM

Professor Bloomer's No-Nonsense Reading Program
Lesson 8

Flash Identification: Procedure, Teacher's Manual Page 46, **(Student Workbook page 29)**
This exercise is primarily a letter discrimination exercise to develop the learner's ability to tell the difference between similar letters.

The letters are flashed for approximately two seconds. The learners are then to underline all the words on that line which have that letter in it. There may be more than one on a line. If the exercise is too difficult, the cards may be flashed for a longer period of time at first, working up to a two second interval or less. Letters forms to Flash. M, W, M, W, W, M.

M	RAW	M AT	RA M	FAR
W	SA W	RAM	MAR	RA W
M	RA M	RAT	SAT	GRASS
W	W AR	FARM	W ARM	SWAM
W	FAT	SAM	SA W	W ARM
M	WAR	WAR M	RAFT	SWA M

Sounds in words: Procedure, Teacher's Manual Page 32, **(Student Workbook page 29)**

The sequence of sounds to be identified are: **/W/, /T/, /R/, /S/, /F/, /W/, /G/, /M/.**

/W/	RAG	W ARM	SAT
/T/	T AGS	SAW	T AR
/R/	WA R	GAS	STA R T
/S/	S TAR	S AW	FAR
/F/	TAG	F AST	MAST
/W/	W AS	STAR	TAG
/G/	ART	G AS	WA G
/M/	RAT	WAR M	SAW

Dictation: Procedure, Teacher's Manual page 16: **(Student Workbook page 29)** **(Use separate lined paper for this exercise)**

Letter/soundS /A/ /T/ /S/. /M/ /R/ /G/ /F/ /W/,
Words:, SAW, WAS, RAW, SWAM, WAR, GRAMA, WARD, DRAW, WARM, STRAW, WAG, START FARM, FAST, WART.

Professor Bloomer's No-Nonsense Reading Program
Lesson 8

WHAT IS THIS? CAN YOU MAKE IT BETTER?

CAN YOU DRAW IT EVEN BETTER DOWN HERE?

Professor Bloomer's No-Nonsense Reading Program
Lesson 8

Drawing Completion Procedure, Teacher's Manual page 48, **(Student Workbook page 38)** is an open ended exercise in developing perceptual and creative abilities. It trains the basic process of inference by requiring our learners to develop a complete object from a few suggestive lines and asks for supportive visual details. This exercise is also good for improving eye-hand coordination. Our goal in this exercise is more stable lines and increased detail.

A. Directions: Look at the sketch in the top box on this page. What do you think it might be? Can you add to it to make it look more realistic. See how good you can make this drawing.

B. Directions: in the box below draw the same figure, See if you can make it even better than the figure you drew the first time.

How many words can you make? Procedure, Teacher's Manual Page 48, **(Student Workbook page 31)**

Directions- On this page are some Letter/sounds. Put them together to make as many words as you can.

The Letter/sounds are   T, R, A, F, W, S, M, G.

Phrases for Writing and Reading Aloud: Procedure, Teacher's Manual page 37-38, **(Student Workbook page 31)** **(Use separate lined paper for this exercise)**

SAM WAS AT A FARM _____
SAM SAW A RAM._____
A RAM SAW GRASS _____
A RAM WAS FAT AND FAST_____
A RAT SAW A SAM _____
SAM SAW A RAT START_____
A RAT SAW A RAFT _____
A RAT WAS FAST _____
A RAT SWAM _____
MAMA SAW A STAR_____
MAMA WAS FAT_____
MAMA WAS WARM _____
SAM SAW A TRAM _____

Professor Bloomer's No-Nonsense Reading Program
Lesson 8

Completing Phrases Procedure, Teacher's Manual page 38-39, **(Student Workbook page 32)** follow the directions in lesson 7.

    SAM WAS __ARM. (W)
    SAM SA__ A RAFT. (W)
    SAM S__AM AT A RAFT.(W)
    MAMA __AW A RAFT (S)
    MAMA SWA__ AT A RA__T (M, F)
    __AMA WAS __ARM. (M, W)
    A __AT RAT S__AM AT A __AFT (F, W, R)

Picture Phrases Procedure, Teacher's Manual Page 21, **(Student Workbook page 32)**

    SAM SAW A RAT, SAM SAW A STAR, SAM SAW FAR, SAM SAT, RATS, ART, FAT, WARM, RAM, FAR, SAWS.

PICTURE PHRASES

SAM SAW A RAT

SAM SAW A STAR

SAM SAW FAR

SAM SAT

Professor Bloomer's No-Nonsense Reading Program
Lesson 8

Professor Bloomer's No-Nonsense Reading Program
Lesson 9

LESSON 9 THE Letter/sound /D/

Purpose. Lesson 9 introduces the Letter/sound /D/ as in dog and related words. The letter D is the first letter in the series which required a special sound review to differentiate it from the letters G and T.

Timing Note: This lesson should take at least THREE sessions preferably separated by a whole day. Teachers should judge by the quality of the learner's responses whether to continue on or to rehearse for a longer period. Resting time between learning sessions for consolidation of learning is essential. Remember to start each session with a Review. Time is not important, Quality is.

Letter/sound /D/. /D/. is made by stopping a column of air with the tip of the tongue pressed against the roof of the mouth and just behind the upper teeth and then releasing it. The release is accompanied by a vibration of the vocal chords. An unvoiced /D/ sounds /T/

Letter formation D
'D' the capital letter 'D' is formed from two lines
    1. The first stroke is a vertical line from the top of the letter to the bottom.

    2. The second stroke curves to the right and proceeds in a single line from the top of the vertical line to the bottom.

Words: ADD, DAD, DAM, DRAM, FAD, WARD, DART, TAD, WAD, MAD, SAD, DRAW .

Beginning Review Procedure, Teachers manual Page 6-7: **(Use separate lined paper for this exercise)**
    Letter/sounds: /A/ /T/ /S/. /M/ /R/ /G/ /F/ /R/ /W/
    Words, SAW, WAS, RAW, SWAM, WAR, WARD, DRAW, WARM, STRAW, WAG, WART., FARM, FAST, RAFT, AFT. GAS, TAG

Introducing the Letter/sound /D/, Procedure: Teacher's Manual page 1;: **(Student Workbook page 34)** The Letter/sound /D/ as in DAD

Professor Bloomer's No-Nonsense Reading Program
Lesson 9

D _____

_____

PICTURES TO LABEL

DAD

MAD

SAD

DART

DRAG

Professor Bloomer's No-Nonsense Reading Program
Lesson 9

Teacher: Now, let's all say /D/ and see how it feels when we say it.

Class: /D/, /D/, /D/.

Teacher: Very good. Now, let's write these letters as I call them out to you. (Teacher calls out the letters in a random fashion and walks about the class being sure that each learner can differentiate and helping those who make errors.) Now let's see if we can write some words with these letters. (Teacher begins special review words, cautioning the learners to listen carefully.

Costructive Synthesis: Procedure: Teacher's Manual page 8; **(Use separate lined paper for this exercise)**

ADD, DAD, DAM, DRAM, FAD, WARD, DART, TAD, WAD, MAD, SAD, DRAW, GRAMA, GRASS

Pictures to Label: Procedure Teacher's Manual page 10: **(Student Workbook page 34)** DAD, MAD, DAD, DRAG, DART.

Match and Label: Procedure, Teacher's Manual page 21: **(Student Workbook page 35)** . Some children may have more trouble than others. Allow the learner to write the label themselves. **FAN, DAM, ANT, RAM, RAN, MAN, SANTA, GRAMA, NAN**

Find the letter and read aloud:. Procedure, Teacher's Manual page 12: **(Student Workbook page 36)**

D	RAFT	FAST	A**DD**
S	TAG**S**	RAW	**S**AM
F	ART	**F**AR	SAT
W	SAT	MAT	**W**ARM
M	**M**AD	RAT	TA**M**
D	WAR	**D**AD	SAT
S	A**S**	FAT	**S**AT
D	SAM	AM	SA**D**

57

Professor Bloomer's No-Nonsense Reading Program
Lesson 9

Matching words: Procedure, Teacher's Manual Page 16, Follow the procedure from Lesson 3 gradually teaching the exercise form and withdrawing to allow learner independence

DAD	DRAG
DAM	SAD
DART	MAD
TAD	TAD
SAD	DAD
DRAG	DART
MAD	DAM

Finding word pairs and Reading aloud: Procedure, Teacher's Manual Page 16, **(Student Workbook page 36)**

DAD	**DAD**	DAM	WARD
DRAM	**SAD**	**SAD**	TAD
MAD	TAD	**MAD**	FAD
DAD	**TAD**	SAD	**TAD**
DART	**WARD**	**WARD**	TAD
DAM	**DAM**	SAM	MAD
SAD	**ADD**	FAD	**ADD**

Flash Identification: Procedure, Teacher's Manual Page 21, **(Student Workbook page 37)** Expose the letters for two (2) seconds Letters to flash: **G, T, D, R, G, T, S, D.**

G	TA**G**	SAD	SA**G**	SAT
T	DRAG	**T**AMS	DRAF**T**	SAM
D	**D**ART	HAT	HA**D**	**D**RAG
R	FAT	DA**R**T	SAG	FA**R**
G	SA**G**	SAD	DRA**G**	TAD
T	DAMS	WAS	HA**T**S	SAM
S	**S**AG	MAT	**S**AW	FAT
D	**D**ART	TAG	TA**D**	**D**RAG

Sounds in words: Procedure, Teacher's Manual page 32 **(Student Workbook page 37)**.

The sequence to use in this lesson is as follow **A, W, M, R, S, D. R, S**

/A/	S**A**G	**A**DD	SW**A**M
/W/	DAM	FAST	**W**AR
/M/	SAD	**M**AD	RAFTS
/R/	G**R**ASS	FAD	SAD
/S/	**S**AG	FAR	DAD
/D/	SAT	TAT	SA**D**
/R/	DA**R**T	GAS	MAST
/S/	FAD	GA**S**	ADD

Professor Bloomer's No-Nonsense Reading Program
Lesson 9

Dictation: Procedure, Teacher's Manual page 16: **(Student Workbook page 37)**

Letter/soundS. /A/ /T/ /S/. /M/ /R/ /G/, /W/, /D/,
Words: ADD, DAD, DAM, DRAM, FAD, WARD, DART, TAD, WAD, MAD, SAD, DRAW GRAMA, GRASS, STAG START, MAST, ART, ARM.

Picture completion: Procedure, Teacher's Manual page 47, **(Student Workbook page 38)**

How many words can you make? Procedure, Teacher's Manual page 32, (**Student Workbook page 39)** Use the procedure from lesson 6.
The Letter/sounds are **D, W, A, S, M, T, R.**

Phrases for Writing and Reading Aloud: Procedure, Teacher's Manual page 37-38, **(Student Workbook page 39) (Use separate lined paper for this exercise)**

DAD WAS MAD. _____
DAD SAW SAM._____
SAM WAS SAD._____
DAD SAW MAMA. _____
MAMA WAS WARM. _____
MAMA WAS MAD AT DAD AND SAM._____
SAM DRAGS A RAFT._____

Professor Bloomer's No-Nonsense Reading Program
Lesson 9

WHAT IS THIS? CAN YOU MAKE IT BETTER?

CAN YOU DRAW IT EVEN BETTER DOWN HERE?

Professor Bloomer's No-Nonsense Reading Program
Lesson 9

Completing Sentences Procedure, Teacher's Manual page 38-39, **(Student Workbook page 40)**

    SAM SA_ A DAR_ (W, T)
    _AMA WAS -ARM (M, W)
    MAMA _AW A RAF_ (S, T)
    MAMA SWA_ AT A RA_T (S, F)
    A _AT RAT S_AM AT A _AFT (R, W, R)

Picture Phrases Procedure, Teacher's Manual Page 21, **(Student Workbook page 41-42)**

SAM, SAM ADDS, SAM RAN AT A RAT., DAN DRAGS A RAFT., TARTS, STRAW, SAD, MAD, DAM, DRAG, TAG, TAM

Professor Bloomer's No-Nonsense Reading Program
Lesson 9

Special Review: Lesson 9 /D/

Special Review, Sound: Letter/sounds /G/ and /T/.
Words. SAD, GAD, SAD, SAT, TAD, .DRAG

Special Review, Shape: Letters G and R.
Words. DART, WARD. DRAG

Sample Sentences and Phrases. SAM WAS MAD. DAD WAS MAD. SAM WAS SAD. DAD WAS SAD. DAD SAW SAM. DAD SAW MAMA. SAM ADDS. DAD ADDS. SAM SAW A DAM. DAD SAW A DAM. MAMA SAW A DAM. MAMA ADDS. MAMA WAS MAD AT DAD. MAMA WAS MAD AT SAM. SAM SAW DAD DRAG A RAFT.

The shape review should begin the review using the procedure in Lesson 8. Letter shape, the visual pattern is more stable than the more fleeting sound This should be followed by a sound and shape combined review of the letter G. The procedure in Unit VI can be used for the phrases and sentences. When the learners are secure with the differentiation of the letter shapes and words begin the sound review,

Procedure: sound review.
Teacher: We have learned about the letter /D/ and some of the words which use /D/. Now let's think carefully and see if we can think of some letters which we have had that sound like /D/.

Class: /T/ and /G/.

Teacher: That's fine, learners. Now, learners, listen very carefully as I write these letters. Let's each say the letters as I write. (Teacher writes T and D several times each, and says the sounds with the class.) Now, I'll call on someone to say the letter I point to. The rest of us will listen carefully and see if we can hear the difference. (Teacher goes about the class asking a learner to say the letter as she points to it.) Let=s see if we can concentrate hard and see how each of the letters feels to us as we say it. (She has the class pronounce T several times.) How does it feel when we say /T/?

Class: You blow on your teeth.

Teacher: That's right. (If the learners do not make this response, the teacher can have the class see it they can feel the blowing on their teeth.) Now, let=s all say /T/ and feel our breaths on our teeth.

Class: /T/. /T/. /T/

Teacher: That's fine. Now, what about /D/? How does it feel when we say /D/?

Class: /D/, /D/, /D/. You can feel it in your throat (neck) and not so much breath on your teeth. (Again, since these are difficult for the learners in the beginning, the teacher may tell the learners what to look for.)

PICTURE PHRASES

SAM

SAM ADDS

SAM RAN AT A RAT

DAN DRAGS A RAFT

Professor Bloomer's No-Nonsense Reading Program
Lesson 9

TARTS

STRAW

SAD

MAD

DAM

DRAG

TAG

TAM

Professor Bloomer's No-Nonsense Reading Program
Lesson 10

LESSON 10 THE Letter/sound /N/

Purpose: Lesson 10 introduces the Letter/sound /N/ as in NOT and words using this letter. The learners continue to grow in understanding the meanings of words both singly and in sentences.

Timing Note: This lesson should take at least THREE sessions preferably separated by s whole day the. Teachers should judge by the quality of the learner's responses whether to continue on or to rehearse for a longer period. Resting time between learning sessions for consolidation of learning is essential. Remember to start each session with a Review. Time is not important, Quality is.

Letter/sound /N/: /N/ is made by opening the lips and closing the mouth with the teeth and tongue. A column of air is pushed out through the nose. This is accompanied by a vibration of the vocal chords. /M/ is made like /N/ with the mouth opened.

Letter formation : **N**
>N= The capital letter >N= is made from three lines.

    1. The first stroke is a vertical line from the top to the bottom of the letter.

    2.. The second stroke is a vertical line from the top to the bottom of the letter. It is made to the right of the initial stroke.

    3. The third stroke angles from the top of the first stroke to the bottom of the second stroke.

Words" AN, AND, ANT, DAN, FAN, GRAND, MAN , NAG, NAN, NAT, RAN, SAND, SANTA, SWAN, TAN, WAND, WANT, WARN.

Beginning Review; Procedure, Teachers manual Page 6-7: **(Use separate lined paper for this exercise)**
    Letter/sounds /A/ /T/ /S/. /M/ /R/ /G/,//W/, /F/, /D/,
    Words ADD, DAD, DAM, DRAM, FAD, WARD, DART, TAD, WAD, MAD, SAD, DRAW

Introducing the Letter/sound /N/, Procedure: Teacher's Manual page 1; **(Student Workbook page 42)**
The Letter/sound /N/ as in NOT

Professor Bloomer's No-Nonsense Reading Program
Lesson 10

N_____

_____

PICTURES TO LABEL

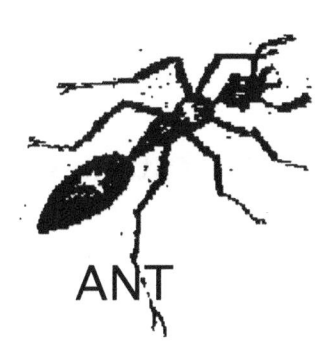
ANT

DAN

SANTA

RAN

FAN

Professor Bloomer's No-Nonsende Reasing Program
Lesson 10

Constructive Synthesis: Procedure: Teacher's Manual page 8; **(Use separate lined paper for this exercise)**

    AN, AND, ANT, DAN, FAN, GRAND, MAN , NAG, NAN, NAT, RAN, SAND, SANTA, SWAN, TAN, WAND, WANT, WARN.

Pictures to Label: Procedure Teacher's Manual page 10: **(Student Workbook page 42)**   **ANT, DAN, DAN RAN. SANTA, FAN, NAN**

Match and label: Procedure, Teacher's Manual page 21: **(Student Workbook page 43)**   **FAN, DAM, RAN, RAM MAN, SANTA, GRAMA, NAN**

Find the letter and reading aloud: Procedure, Teacher's Manual page 12: **(Student Workbook page 44)**

N	A**N**TS	A**N**	TAG
D	**D**ART	SAW	AN**D**
R	SAND	**R**AN	FAST
F	**F**ANS	RAT	NAT
N	A**N**D	STAR	DA**N**
G	ART	**G**RASS	TA**G**S
W	TAN	**W**ANT	SAND
N	A**N**TS	WAR	**N**A**N**

Matching words: Procedure, Teacher's Manual page 16: **(Student Workbook page 44)**

AN	ANT
ANT	DAN
DAN	AND
FAN	AN
AND	WANT
WANT	FAN

MATCH AND LABEL

FAN
DAM
ANT
RAM
RAN
MAN
SANTA
GRAMA
NAN

Professor Bloomer's No-Nonsense Reading Program
Lesson 10

Finding word pairs and Reading aloud: Procedure, Teacher's Manual page 16: **(Student Workbook page 45)**

SAM	**WANT**	SWAN	**WANT**
SAND	**SAND**	SAT	MAT
NAT	WAND	**ANT**	**ANT**
AND	TAN	SWAN	**AND**
TAN	**AN**	**AN**	FAN
DAN	**DAN**	NAG	AN
TAN	SWAN	**FAN**	**FAN**
WAND	NAN	**WAND**	SAND
WANT	RAN	SAM	RAN
SWAN	SWAN	TAN	WAND

Flash Identification. Procedure, Teacher's Manual page 46, **(Student Workbook page 45)**
Expose the letters for two (2) seconds Letters to Flash are: **U, A, N, D, M, W, U, A**.

U	M**U**ST	MAST	AS	WAS
A	FUR	SUM	RUG	F**A**R
N	**N**UT	MUD	SWUM	FU**N**
D	TUG	**D**AN	**D**UG	MU**D**
M	**M**UST	SA**M**	SUN	FAR
W	FAR	S**W**AM	MUM	MAM
U	MAD	F**U**N	M**U**D	AS
A	SUM	RAT	TUG	SAM

Sounds in words: Procedure, Teacher's Manual page 32, **(Student Workbook page 46)**
The sequence to use in this lesson is **S, T, R, M, S, F, G, W.**

/S/	NAN	WANT**S**	DART**S**
/T/	SAN**T**A	DAN	WAN**T**
/R/	**R**AT	WAND	**R**AN
/M/	AND	MAN	**M**ART
/S/	WAG	GRA**SS**	ANT**S**
/F/	DAN	**F**AN	SAND
/G/	MAD	SAND	**G**AS
/W/	**W**ANT	**W**ARD	SAM

Professor Bloomer's No-Nonsense Reading Program
Lesson 10

Dictation: Procedure, Teacher's Manual page 12: **(Student Workbook page 46) (Use separate lined paper for this exercise)**

    Letter/soundS, /A/ /T/ /S/. /M/ /R/ /G/ , /F/, /W/, /D/, /N/
    Words: AN, AND, ANT, DAN, FAN, GRAND, MAN , NAG, NAN, NAT, RAN, SAND, SANTA, SWAN, TAN, WAND, WANT, WARN.

How many words can you make? Procedure, Teacher's Manual page 32, **((Student Workbook page 46)**

The Letter/sounds are **D. S. N. R, T, F, A.**

Picture completion: Procedure, Teacher's Manual page 46, **(Student Workbook page 47)**

Phrases to Read Aloud and Write Procedure, Teacher's Manual page 37-38, **(Student Workbook page 48) (Use separate lined paper for this exercise)**

    NAN SAW ANTS_____
    DAN SAW A SWAN_____
    NAN AND NAT RAN_____
    DAN SAW A TAN RAT_____
    A TAN RAT WANTS A TART_____
    MAMA WAS WARM_____
    MAMA WANTS A FAN_____
    NAN AND DAN SAW MAMA FAN_____

Completing Phrases: Procedure, Teacher's Manual page 38-39, **(Student Workbook page 48)** t

    A RAT RA_ (R)
    DAD SAW A' FA_ . (N)
    NAT S_W SA_TA. (A, N)
    A RA_ AND A_ ANT SWAM. (T, N)
    DAD SA_ A MAN AND A SWA_. (W, N)
    A S_AN SWAM FA_T. (W, S)
    A _AM RAN AT D_N. (R, A)

10. WHAT IS THIS? CAN YOU MAKE IT BETTER?

CAN YOU DRAW IT EVEN BETTER DOWN HERE?

Professor Bloomer's No-Nonsense Reading Program
Lesson 10

Special Review: Lesson 11
ULetters. Review for sound: A, U.

Words. Review for sound: DRAG DRUG, DRAM DRUM, FAN FUN, FUR FAR, JUG JAG, MUD MAD, MUST MAST, NUT NAT, RUG RAG, RUN RAN, TAG TUG.

Phrases and sentences: A RAT MUST RUN FAST. SAM SAW NAN DUST A MUG AND A JAR. A RAT DUG A NUT. SAM MUST TUG A RAFT. DAN MUST ADD A SUM. SAM SAW US RUN. NAN DUG SAND. NAN WAS FUN. A MAN SAW US RUN FAST. A RAT SAW A NUT. A RAT SAW US AND RAN FAR. A FAT MUTT RAN AT A RAT. SAM SAW. DAN AND NAN JUST SAW A RAFT.

Picture Phrases: Procedure, Teacher's Manual page 21: **(Student Workbook page 49)**

SAM RAN. SAM RAN AT A RAT. DAN AND NAN RAN. SAM SAW AN ANT. FAN MAMA. DAN AND NAN SAW A RAT.   SAM SAW A SWAN. SAM SAW DAD.

PICTURE PHRASES

DAN RAN

DAN RAN AT A RAT

PICTURE PHRASES

DAN AND NAN RAN

SAM SAW AN ANT

DAD FANS MAMA

DAN RAN AT A RAT

DAN SAW A SWAN

DAN AND NAN SAW A RAT

DAN

SAW

DAD

Professor Bloomer's No-Nonsense Reading Program
Lesson 11

LESSON 11 THE VOWEL Letter/sound /U/

Purpose. Unit XII introduces the VOWEL Letter/sound /U/ AS IN BUG. The learners continue to build understanding through additional words, phrases and sentences, made possible by the introduction of a new vowel sound.

Timing Note: This lesson shgould take at least THREE sessions preferably separated by a whole day. Teachers should judge by the quality of the learner's responses whether to continue on or to rehearse for a longer period. Resting time between learning sessions for consolidation of learning is essential. Remember to start each session with a Review. Time is not important, Quality is.

Letter/sound. /U/.as in BUG, /U/ is formed high and back in the mouth. The lips are not rounded, and are not tense. /U/ is a voiced sound.

Letter formation U
U The capital letter U is made from three lines

1. The first stroke is a vertical line starting at the top of the letter and proceeding four fifths of the way to the bottom of the letter.
2. The second stroke is a curved line that proceeds from the bottom of the initial stroke to the right
3. The third stroke is a vertical line starting at the top of the letter and proceeding straight down to join the end of the second stroke

Words. DRUM, DUN, DUST, FUN, FUR, FUSS, GUM, GUN, GUS, GUST, MUD, MUG, MUM, MUST, MUTT, NUN, NUT, RUG, RUN, RUST, RUT, HUNT, SUM, SUN, SNUG, STUD, STRUM, SWUM, TRUST, TUG, TURN, US.

Procedure. The letter is introduced following the procedure described in Unit IV. Special Review for sound follows the procedure of Unit VIII. Phrases and sentences follow the procedure of Unit VI.

Comments. Care should be taken not to introduce the letter A initially while the learners are learning the letter U. The learners should only be exposed to learning the one vowel at a time to avoid confusion. Be sure that each learner learns not only the sound of the letter U, but the shape also, before attempting the Special Review. The better the U is learned, the more successful and rapid the Special Review will be. Teacher shows word cards, and the learners use the words in sentences. Try and see how many sentences can be added to the language book using one or another words.

Professor Bloomer's No-Nonsense Reading Program
Lesson 11

Beginning Review: Procedure, Teachers manual Page 6-7: **(Use separate lined paper for this exercise)**

    Letter/sounds /A/ /T/ /S/. /M/ /R/ /G/ , /F/, /W/, /D/, /N/
    Words: AN, AND, ANT, DAN, FAN, GRAND, MAN , NAG, NAN, NAT, RAN, SAND, SANTA,   SWAN, TAN, WAND, WANT, WARN.

Introducing the Letter/sound /U/, Procedure: Teacher's Manual page 1;**(Student Workbook page 50)**
The Letter/sound /U/ as in UP

ConstructiveSynthesis: Procedure: Teacher's Manual page 8; for the words DRUM, DUN, DUST, FUN, FUR, FUSS, GUM, GUN, GUS, GUST, MUD, MUG, MUM, MUST, MUTT, NUN, NUT, RUG, RUN, RUST, RUT, HUNT, SUM, SUN, SNUG, STUD, STRUM, SWUM, TRUST, TUG, TURN, US. Remember to attach the vowel to the initial consonant sound for best results in blending.

Pictures to Label: Procedure Teacher's Manual page 10: **(Student Workbook page 50)**   SUN, TUG, RUN, RUG, DRUM, DUST

Match and Label: Procedure, Teacher's Manual page 21: **(Student Workbook page 51)**
    DRUM, SUN, FARM, RAT, FUN, DUG, NUT, FAN, TAG, DUST

Find the letter and reading aloud. Procedure, Teacher's Manual page 12: **(Student Workbook page 52)**

G	DU**G**	RUN	SWUM
R	**R**UT	SUM	FU**R**
M	GUST	**M**UST	DUST
D	RUST	MUG	**D**UST
G	**G**UN	NUT	**G**US
N	**N**UT	RUST	RU**N**
T	GUN	RU**T**	**T**UG
S	FUN	**S**UN	DU**S**T

Professor Bloomer's No-Nonsense Reading Program
Lesson 11

U _____

_____

PICTURES TO LABEL

SUN

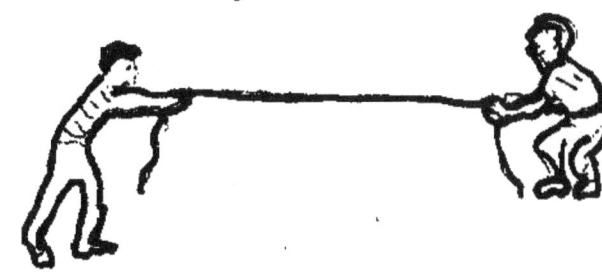
TUG

RUN

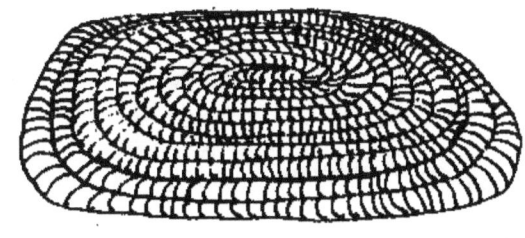
RUG

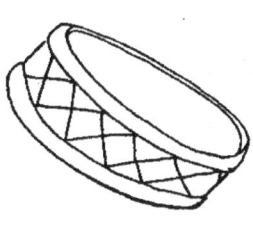
DRUM

DUST

MATCH AND LABEL

Professor Bloomer's No-Nonsense Reading Program
Lesson 11

Matching words: Procedure, Teacher's Manual page 16: **(Student Workbook page 52)** Follow the procedure from Lesson 3 gradually teaching the exercise form and withdrawing to allow learner independence

DRUM	FUN
FUN	TRUST
GUM	DRUM
MUST	US
RUN	GUM
SUN	MUST
TRUST	RUN
US	SUN

Finding word pairs and reading aloud: Procedure, Teacher's Manual page 16: **(Student Workbook page 53)**

DRUM	**DRUM**	FUR	RUT
FUN	ADD	**FUN**	RUN
NUT	**MUD**	**MUD**	ANT
RUG	FUR	SUM	**RUG**
RUT	**GUN**	**GUN**	TUG
MUST	**NUT**	MAD	**NUT**
DAN	**RUN**	**RUN**	FUR
SUN	NUT	RUN	**SUN**
FUR	NUT	**DUST**	**DUST**
MUST	RUT	TUG	**MUST**

Flash Identification: Procedure, Teacher's Manual page 46. **(Student Workbok page 53)**
Letters to Flash are **H, J, G, T, N, J. F, G.**

H	**H**AM	FAN	JAM	**H**ARM
J	RUST	**J**UST	MUST	DUST
G	**G**AS	JAR	JU**G**	DART
T	JU**T**	MA**T**	HU**T**	**T**AD
N	FA**N**	JAW	RAW	JA**N**
J	**J**AM	**J**AR	**J**AN	**J**AW
F	JAM	**F**AN	**F**AT	JAN
G	JUT	DRA**G**	JU**G**	HAD

Professor Bloomer's No-Nonsense Reading Program
Lesson 11

Sounds in words; Procedure, Teacher's Manual page 32, **(Student Workbook page 54)** Letter/sounds to be spoken: U, D, N, U, A, T, U, S.

/U/	DRAM	G**U**ST	SAND	MAN	DR**U**M
/D/	MUST	SWAM	NAN	SAN**D**	TAR
/N/	DAM	DUST	MUT	SUM	SU**N**
/U/	D**U**ST	D**U**G	WANT	RAFT	RAN
/A/	MUTT	R**A**G	RUST	R**A**W	RUN
/T/	**T**UG	WARD	**T**AN	MAN	WAN**T**
/U/	DART	SANTA	SWUM	**U**S	RAN
/S/	AN	TRU**S**T	MAD	**S**AT	GUN**S**

Dictation: Procedure, Teacher's Manual page 16: **(Student Workbook page 54)** **(Use separate lined paper for this exercise)**

Letter/soundS, /A/ /T/ /S/. /M/ /R/ /G/., / W/, /R/ /N/ /U/.
Words: DRUM, DUN, DUST, FUN, FUR, FUSS, GUM, GUN, GUS, GUST, MUD, MUG, MUM, MUST, MUTT, NUN, NUT, RUG, RUN, RUST, RUT, HUNT, SUM, SUN, SNUG, STUD, STRUM, SWUM, TRUST, TUG, TURN, US.

Picture completion: Procedure, Teacher's Manual page 46, **(Student Workbook page 55)**

How many words can you make? Procedure, Teacher's Manual page 32, **(Student Workbook page 54)** .
The Letter/sounds are: **G, S, T, N, U, D, R, A.**

Professor Bloomer's No-Nonsense Reading Program
Lesson 11

10. WHAT IS THIS? CAN YOU MAKE IT BETTER?

CAN YOU DRAW IT EVEN BETTER DOWN HERE?

Professor Bloomer's No-Nonsense Reading Program
Lesson 11

Phrases to Read Aloud and Write: Procedure, Teacher's Manual page 37-38, **(Student Workbook page 56) (Use separate lined paper for this exercise)**

    NAN SAW A DRUM_____
    DAN SAW A GUN._____
    A RAT MUST RUN FAST. _____
    DAN SAW NAN DUST A MUG._____
    SAM MUST TUG AND DRAG A RAFT._____
    A FARM WAS FUN. _____
    A RAT DUG A NUT. _____
    DAD SAW US RUN FAST. _____
    DAN MUST DUST A RUG._____

Completing Phrases: Procedure, Teacher's Manual page 38-39, **(Student Workbook page 56)**

    A FLAT RA**F**T HAD A TA**LL** MAST. (F, LL)
    A **L**AD HAD A SA**L**AD. (L, L)
    DAN RAN L**A**ST. (A)
    A FARM HAD **H**ARD **L**AND. (H, L)
    DAN HAD A FLA**G**. (G)

Pictures Phrases: Picture Phrases: Procedure, Teacher's Manual page 21: **(Student Workbook page 56-57)**

SAM DRUMS. DAD HAS A GUN, NUTS, SUN, GUN, DRUM GRAMA TATS, GUM A MAN DUG, DUST, FUR.

Professor Bloomer's No-Nonsense Reading Program
Lesson 11

Special Review: Lesson 11
U - Letters. Review for sound: A, U.

Words. Review for sound: DRAG DRUG, DRAM DRUM, FAN FUN, FUR FAR, JUG JAG, MUD MAD, MUST MAST, NUT NAT, RUG RAG, RUN RAN, TAG TUG.

Phrases and sentences: A RAT MUST RUN FAST. SAM SAW NAN DUST A MUG AND A JAR. A RAT DUG A NUT. SAM MUST TUG A RAFT. DAN MUST ADD A SUM. SAM SAW US RUN. NAN DUG SAND. NAN WAS FUN. A MAN SAW US RUN FAST. A RAT SAW A NUT. A RAT SAW US AND RAN FAR. A FAT MUTT RAN AT A RAT. SAM SAW. DAN AND NAN JUST SAW A RAFT.

Procedure. Follow the procedure in Lesson 8 as before. The discrimination between vowels is very important for the learners.

DAN DRUMS   DADS GUN

PICTURE PHRASES

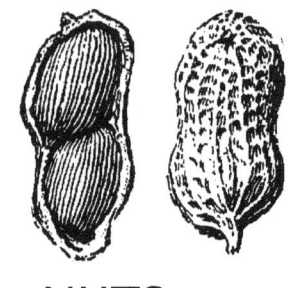
NUTS

SUN

GUN

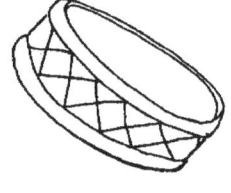
DRUM

GUM

GRAMA TATS

FUR

DUST

A MAN DUG

Professor Bloomer's No-Nonsense Reading Program
Lesson 12

LESSON 12 THE Letter/sound /H/

Purpose. The Letter/sound /H/ AS IN HAT is introduced, and discrimination of the two vowel sounds (A and U) is continued.

Timing Note: This lesson should take at least THREE sessions preferably separated by a whole day. Teachers should judge by the quality of the learner=s responses whether to continue on or to rehearse for a longer period. Resting time between learning sessions for consolidation of learning is essential. Remember to start each session with a Review. Time is not important, Quality is.

Letter/sound. /H/. AS IN HAT. /H/ the letter H is made by blowing a breath through the open mouth. /H/ is formed by partially constricting the throat and forcing out a column of air. /H/ does not require vibration of the vocal chords. A voiced /H/ sounds like /A/.

Letter formation
>H The capital letter "H" is made from three straight lines.

1. The first stroke is a vertical line from the top to the bottom of the letter.
2. The second stroke is a vertical line from the top to the bottom of the letter. It is made to the right of the initial stroke.
3. The third stroke is a horizontal line connecting the middle of the first two stokes.

Words. HAT, HAD, HAM, HAND, HARD, HARM, HAS, HAT, HUG, HUM, HURT, HUT, HUNT.

Beginning Review: Procedure, Teachers manual Page 6-7: **(Use separate lined paper for this exercise)**
Letter/sounds /A/ /T/ /S/. /M/ /R/ /G/./F/, /W/, /R/ /N/ /U/.
Words: DRUM, DUN, DUST, FUN, FUR, FUSS, GUM, GUN, GUS, GUST, MUD, MUG, MUM, MUST, MUTT, NUN, NUT, RUG, RUN, RUST, RUT, HUNT, SUM, SUN, SNUG, STUD, STRUM, SWUM, TRUST, TUG,

Introducing the Letter/sound /H/, Procedure: Teacher's Manual page 1;**(Student Workbook page 58)**
The Letter/sound /H/ as in HOT i

Professor Bloomer's No-Nonsense Reading Program
Lesson 12

Constructive Synthesis: Procedure: Teacher's Manual page 8; f **(Use separate lined paper for this exercise)**

HAT, HAD, HAM, HAND, HARD, HARM, HAS, HAT, HUG, HUM, HURT, HUT, HUNT.

Pictures to Label: Procedure Teacher's Manual page 10: **(Student Workbook page 58)**
HUT, HURT, HAT, HUNT, HUG, HAM

Match and Label: Procedure, Teacher's Manual page 21: **(Student Workbook page 59)** HAM, HAT, HUT, HAND, HURT, FARM, DRUM, HARD, NUT, HAMMERS

Find the letter and read aloud: Procedure, Teacher's Manual page 12: **(Student Workbook page 60)**

Find the Letter H, M, N, D. H, R, T, H.

H	**H**AM	SAD	WARM
M	SA**M**	HA**M**	HAD
N	HA**N**D	FAR	HARM
D	HA**D**	HAR**D**	HUM
H	STAR	ART	**H**AT
R	HU**R**T	AS	HAS
T	HAND	HU**T**	RAM
H	**H**AD	TAR	**H**AT

Matching words: Procedure, Teacher's Manual page 16: **(Student Workbook page 60)**

HAM	HUT
HARD	HAM
HURT	HUG
HUG	HARD
HAS	HAS
HAND	HAD
HUT	HAND
HAD	HURT

Professor Bloomer's No-Nonsense Reading Program
Lesson 12

_____

_____

PICTURES TO LABEL

A HUT

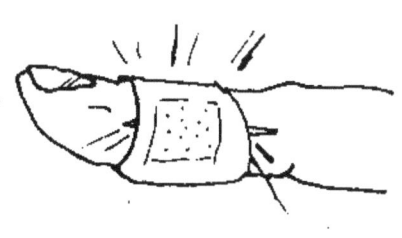

HURT

HAT

A MAN HUNTS

MAMA HUGS

HAM

MATCH AND LABEL

HAM
HAT
HUT
HAND
HURT
FARM
DRUM
HARD
NUTS
HAMMERS

HAT

HUT

HAND

FARM

HAND

HARD

HURT

DAN DRUMS

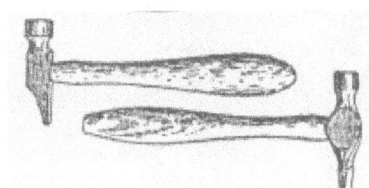
HAMMERS

HAM

NUTS

Professor Bloomer's No-Nonsense Reading Program
Lesson 12

Finding word pairs and reading aloud: Procedure, Teacher's Manual page 16: **(Student Workbook page 61)**

HURT	HUT	HAD	**HURT**
HAM	**HAND**	**HAND**	HARM
HAD	HURT	**HAD**	HAS
HUM	**HARD**	**HARD**	HAT
HAND	**HAM**	HURT	**HAM**
HUT	HAD	**HUT**	HAS
HUM	**HUM**	HAND	HARD
HAS	HURT	**HARM**	**HARM**
HUG	HAM	**HUG**	HAD
HAD	**HAS**	**HAS**	HAND

Flash Identification: Procedure, Teacher's Manual page 46: **(Student Workbook page 61)**
Expose the letters for two (2) seconds Letters to Flash are: M, H, N, A, F, H, U, H.

M	HAR**M**	HAD	**M**AD	RAW
H	FARM	**H**ARM	**H**AT	DUG
N	**S**UM	**S**UN	HARM	HAND
A	HUM	HUT	H**A**T	H**A**M
F	**F**AT	HAS	**F**AST	HAT
H	FAN	NAT	**H**ARD	DART
U	H**U**T	H**U**RT	HAD	H**U**M
H	FAST	**H**AD	MAD	TAD

Sounds in words: Procedure, Teacher's Manual page 32: **(Student Workbook page 62)** The sequence of Letter/sounds to use in this lesson is as follow /H/, /U/, /D/, /H/, /N/, /U/, /H/, /S/.

/H/	AND	**H**AD	DUST	**H**UM	DART
/U/	D**U**N	H**U**G	MAST	F**U**N	SAND
/D/	RAN	HA**D**	GUST	HAN**D**	NUT
/H/	DAD	**H**URT	**H**ARM	SWARM	**H**AM
/N/	HAM	MA**N**	DRAG	HA**N**D	GU**N**
/U/	HAT	SAD	H**U**RT	HARM	D**U**G
/H/	WAS	HAS	**H**UM	NUT	**H**UT
/S/	RAN	**S**AW	DRAM	HA**S**	AND

Dictation: Procedure, Teacher's Manual page 16: **(Student Workbook page 62)**, **(Use separate lined paper for this exercise)**

Letter/sounds, /A/ /T/ /S/. /M/ /R/ /G/./F/, /W/, /R/ /N/ /U/, /H/
WORDS: HAT, HAD, HAM, HAND, HARD, HARM, HAS, HAT, HUG, HUM, HURT, HUT, HUNT.

89

Professor Bloomer's No-Nonsense Reading Program
Lesson 12

How many words can you make? Procedure, Teacher's Manual page 32: **(Student Workbook page 62)** .
The Letter/sounds are **H, A, N, U, R, D, R, T**

Picture completion: Procedure, Teacher's Manual page 47:
(Student Workbook page 63)

Phrases to Read and Write: Procedure, Teacher's Manual page 37-38: **(Student Workbook page 64) (Use separate lined paper for this exercise)**

A RAT HAD A HAM_____
RUST HURTS A GUN_____
A RAT HAS TAN FUR_____
DAN HAD A HURT HAND_____
DADS HAT WAS MUD AND SAND_____
MAMA HUGS SAM_____
HARD TAR HURT NAN_____
A RAM CAN HARM SAM_____

Completing Phrases: Procedure, Teacher's Manual page 38-39 **(Student Workbook page 64)** .

A RAT **H**AS TAN FUR. (H)
DAN'S **H**AND **W**AS HURT. (H, W)
MAMA H**U**GS SAM. (H)
A RAT HAD A H**A**M. (A)
A RAM CAN **H**ARM SAM. (H)

Picture Phrases: Picture Phrases: Procedure, Teacher's Manual page 21:
(Student Workbook page 65) (Use separate lined paper for this exercise)

HUT, A WARM MUFF, DAN HAS A FAN, GUN, DAD DUSTS A HAT. A RAT HAS A HAM, NUTS, A HARD HAND. DAN AND DAD HUNT.

Professor Bloomer's No-Nonsense Reading Program
Lesson 12

10. WHAT IS THIS? CAN YOU MAKE IT BETTER?

CAN YOU DRAW IT EVEN BETTER DOWN HERE?

Special Review: Lesson 12
Procedure: follow the procedure in lesson 9 for shape review and Lesson 8 for sound review

Letters. Review for sounds: A. Review for shape: F.

Words. Review for sound: FAT, HAT, FARM, HARM, HAD, FAD.

Review for shape: FARM, HARM, HAD, FAD.

Sentences and Phrases: A RAT HAD A TART. SAM HAD A FUR HAT. DAN HAD A NUT. NAN AND DAN HAD A WAR. AND NAN WAS HURT. MAMA HUGS SAM AND NAN. A RAT HAS TAN FUR. RUST HURTS A GUN. SAM HAS GUM. MAMA HAD A FAN. SAM AND DAN HAD FERN AT A HUT. DAN WAS HURT AND MAMA WAS SAD. A RAT HARMS A TART.

PICTURE PHRASES

HUT

A WARM MUFF

DAN HAS A FAN

GUN

DAD DUSTS A HAT

A RAT HAS A HAM

NUTS

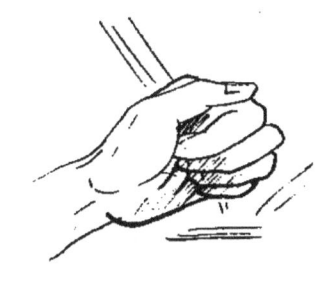
A HARD HAND

DAN AND DAD HUNT

Professor Bloomer's No-Nonsense Reading Program
Lesson 13

LESSON 13 THE Letter/sound /J/

Purpose. Lesson 13 introduces the Letter/sound /J/ as in JUST and some additional words. The learners continue to develop skills in understanding through new words, phrases and sentences.

Timing Note: This lesson should take at least THREE sessions preferably separated by s whole day the. Teachers should judge by the quality of the learner=s responses whether to continue on or to rehearse for a longer period. Resting time between learning sessions for consolidation of learning is essential. Remember to start each session with a Review. Time is not important, Quality is.

Letter/sound. /J/ as in JUST. /J/ is formed by stopping a column of air with the tongue against the roof of the mouth just behind the upper front teeth.

Letter formation J

The capital letter >J= is made from two lines.

    1. The first stroke is a vertical line starting at the top of the letter and proceeding four fifths of the way to the bottom of the letter.

    2. The second stroke is a curved line that proceeds from the bottom of the initial stroke to the left

Words. JAM, JAN, JAR, JAG JAW, JUST, JUT.

Beginning Review: Procedure, Teachers manual Page 6-7: **(Use separate lined paper for this exercise)**
    Letter/sounds: /A/ /T/ /S/. /M/ /R/ /G/./F/, /W/, /R/ /N/ /U/, /H/
    Words: HAT, HAD, HAM, HAND, HARD, HARM, HAS, HAT, HUG, HUM, HURT, HUT, HUNT.

Introducing the Letter/sound /J/, Procedure: Teacher's Manual page 1; **(Student Workbook page 66)**
The Letter/sound /J/ as in JET.

J

PICTURES TO LABEL

JAM JAR

JAM TART

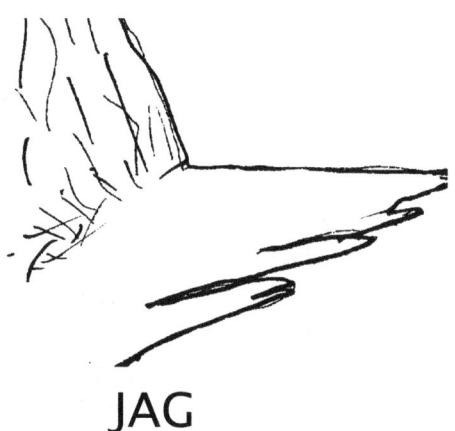

JAG

JUG

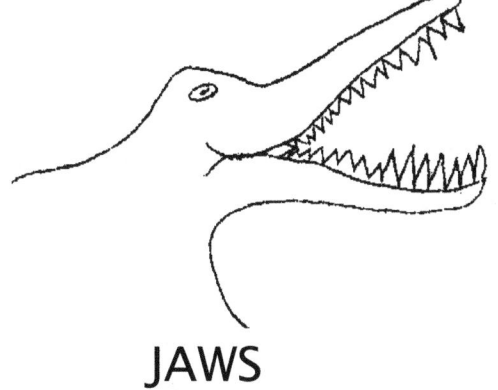

JAWS

Professor Bloomer's No-Nonsense Reading Program
Lesson 13

Constructive Synthesis: Procedure: Teacher's Manual page 8; **(Use separate lined paper for this exercise)**

JAM, JAN, JAR, JAW, JUST, JUT, HAND, HARD, HARM, HAS, HAT, HUG, HUM, HURT,

Pictures to Label: Procedure Teacher's Manual page 10: **(Student Workbook page 66)**
JAM JAR, JAM TART JUG, JAG JAW.

Match and Label: Procedure, Teacher's Manual page 21: **(Student Workbook page 67)**
The teacher will continue to help learners as needed. But allowing the child to write the label themselves. **JAM, HATS, JUG, HUG, HUT, JAG, JAW, WAR, JAR, GUST.**

Find the letter. Procedure, Teacher's Manual page 16: **(Student Workbook page 68)**

J	**J**AR	SAM	**J**AN
N	STAR	FAR	**N**UT
A	MUD	J**A**M	SAT
W	JA**W**	TUG	**W**AG
T	RU**T**	NAN	JU**T**
J	**J**UST	DAM	MUST
U	MAD	J**U**G	ART
R	JA**R**	DAN	**R**UN

Matching words: Procedure, Teacher's Manual page 12: **(Student Workbook page 68).**

JUT	JAM
JAM	JAW
JAR	JUT
JAW	JUST
JUST	JAN
JAN	JAR

Professor Bloomer's No-Nonsense Reading Program
Lesson 13

MATCH AND LABEL

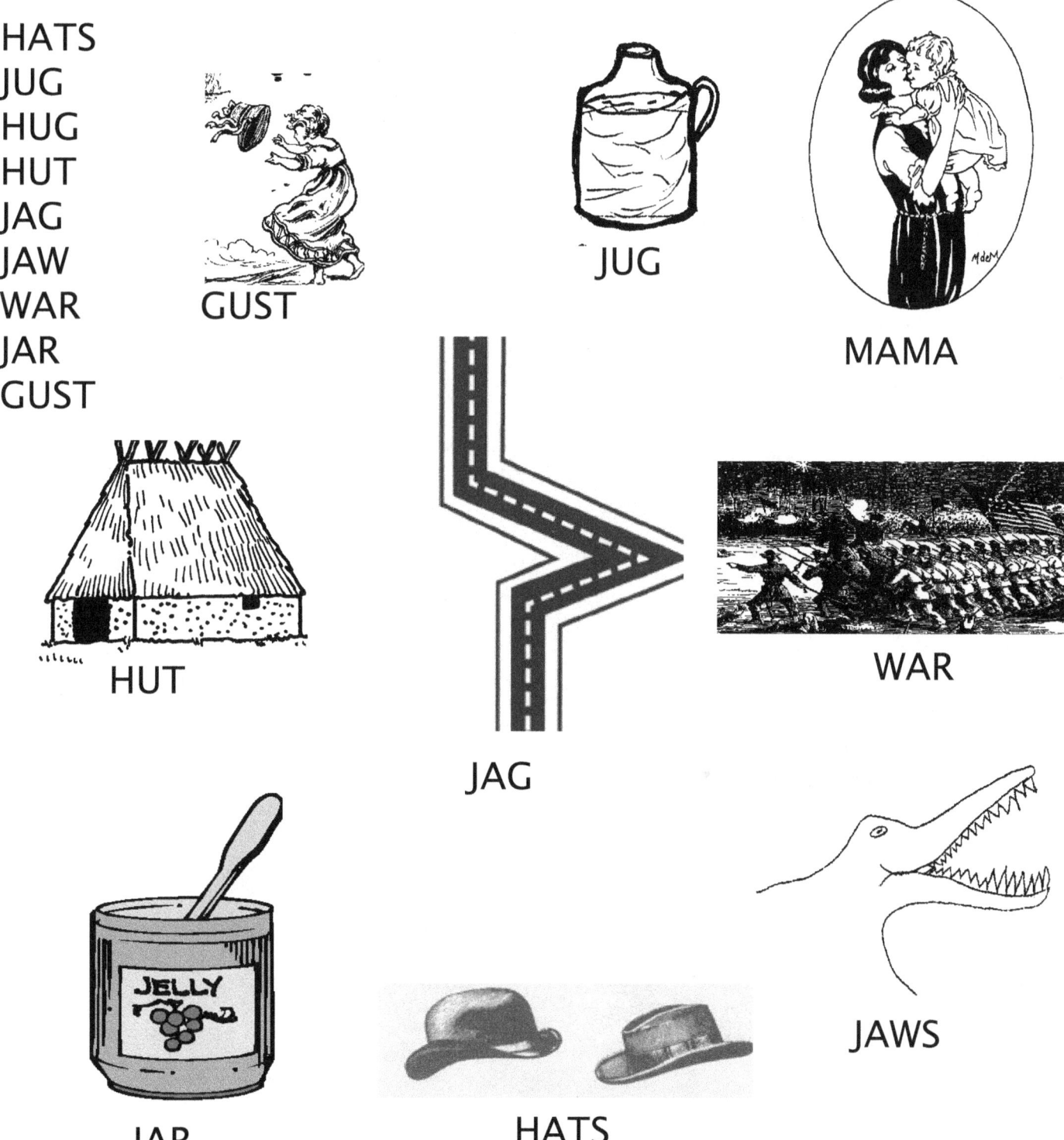

HATS
JUG
HUG
HUT
JAG
JAW
WAR
JAR
GUST

GUST

JUG

MAMA

HUT

JAG

WAR

JAR

HATS

JAWS

Professor Bloomer's No-Nonsense Reading Program
Lesson 13

Finding word pairs and reading aloud: Procedure, Teacher's Manual page 16: **(Student Workbook page 69)**

JAW	MAT	**JAW**	JUST
JUT	**JUG**	**JUG**	JAM
JUST	SAM	JUG	**JUST**
JUT	**JUT**	RUT	JUG
JAG	JAM	JAN	**JAG**
JUST	JAG	**JAN**	**JAN**
JAR	JUT	**JAR**	HAM
JAW	**JAM**	**JAM**	JAR

Flash Identification: Procedure, Teacher's Manual page 47: **(Student Workbook page 69)** Expose the letters for two (2) seconds
Letters to Flash are **H, J, G, T, N, J. F, G.**

H	**H**AM	FAN	JAM	**H**ARM
J	RUST	**J**UST	MUST	DUST
G	**G**AS	JAR	JU**G**	DART
T	JU**T**	MA**T**	HU**T**	**T**AD
N	FA**N**	JAW	RAW	JA**N**
J	**J**AM	**J**AR	**J**AN	**J**AW
F	JAM	**F**AN	**F**AT	JAN
G	JUT	DRA**G**	JU**G**	HAD

Sounds in words: Procedure, Teacher's Manual page 32: **(Student Workbook page 70)**
The sequence of Letter/sounds to use in this lesson is as follow
/J/, /W/, /M/, /D/, /F/, /G/, /R/, /J/.

/J/	MAD	**J**AM	DRAM	WAS
/W/	JA**W**	FAD	GRASS	ADD
/M/	JA**M**	WAR**M**	**M**AD	TAD
/D/	JAW	WAG	A**DD**	**D**ART
/F/	**F**AD	SAW	MAD	RA**F**T
/G/	DAM	**G**AS	JAR	SAW
/R/	MAD	JA**R**	**R**AM	SAT
/J/	SAD	FAST	**J**AR	WAS

Dictation: Procedure, Teacher's Manual page 16: **(Student Workbook page 70)** **(Use separate lined paper for this exercise)**

Letter/soundS /A/ /T/ /S/. /M/ /R/ /G/./F/, /W/, /R/ /N/ /U/, /H/ /J/
and the WORDS JAM, JAN, JAR, JAW, JUST, JUT, HAND, HARD, HARM, HAS, HAT, **HUG, HUM, HURT,**

Professor Bloomer's No-Nonsense Reading Program
Lesson 13

10. WHAT IS THIS? CAN YOU MAKE IT BETTER?

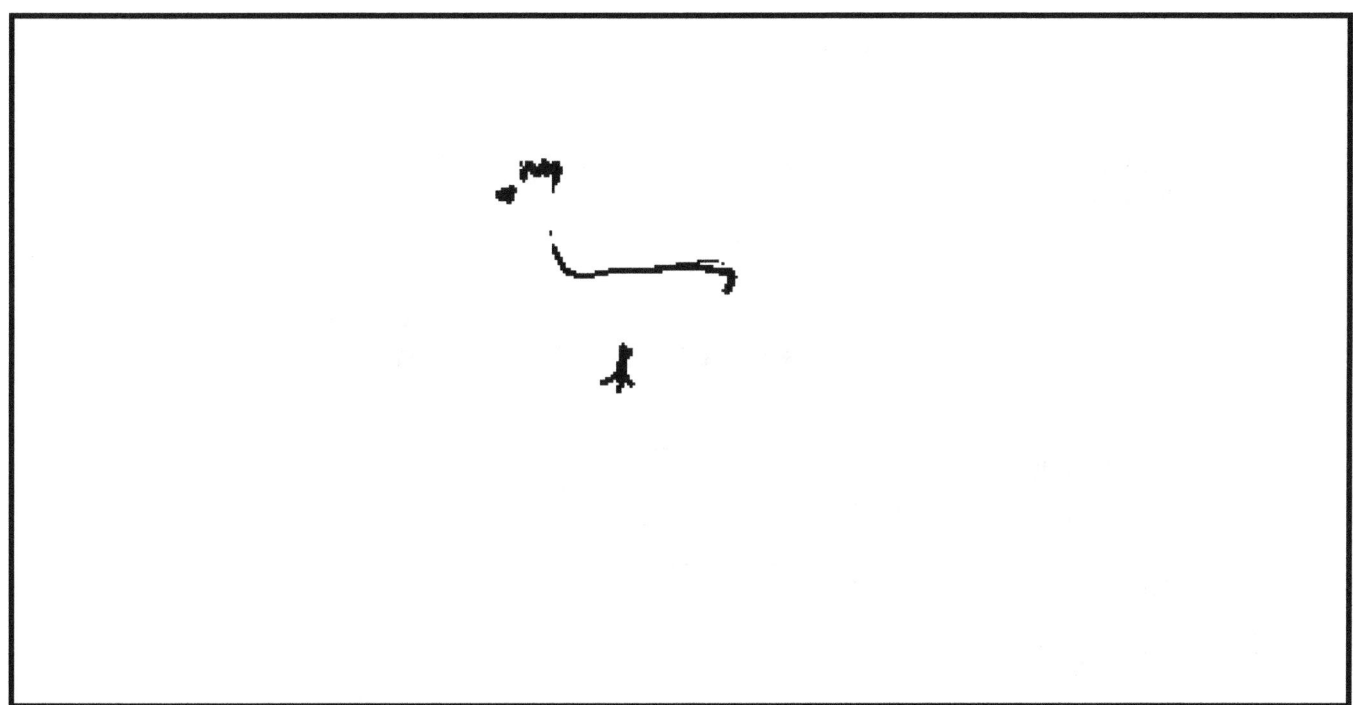

CAN YOU DRAW IT EVEN BETTER DOWN HERE?

Professor Bloomer's No-Nonsense Reading Program
Lesson 13

How many words can you make? Procedure, Teacher's Manual page 32: **(Student Workbook page 70)** allows the learners to practice their synthesis skills.

. The Letter/sounds are **J. U, A, S, T. M. R. H**

Picture completion: Procedure, Teacher's Manual page 47: **(Student Workbook page 71)**

Phrases to Read and Write: Procedure, Teacher's Manual page 37-38: **(Student Workbook page 72) (Use separate lined paper for this exercise)**

    AN ANT SAT AT A JAM JAR _____
JAN DUSTS A JUG._____
A RAT JUST HAD A JAM TART._____
A HARD JUT HURT SAM=S JAW._____
A RAT SAT AT A JAM JAR._____
SAM SAW A JAM JAR. _____
JAN JUST RAN, AND RAN FAST_____

Completing Phrases: Procedure, Teacher's Manual page 38-39: **(Student Workbook page 72**

    JAN D**U**STS A JU**G**. (U, G)
A RAT **J**UST HAD A **J**AM TART. (J, J)
SAM HAS A **J**UG (J)
SAM WANTS A **J**AM JAR. (J)
NAN **J**UST HAD A J**A**M TART (J, A)

Pictures phrases: Procedure, Teacher's Manual page 21: **(Student Workbook page 72-73)**

    SAM HAD JAM AND HAM, AN ANT AT A JAM JAR. SAM RAM AT A JAM JAR, GRAMA HUGS SAM. JAM JAR

PICTURE PHRASES

DAN RAN AT A JAM JAR

GRAMA HUGS DAN

A JAM JAR

Professor Bloomer's No-Nonsense Reading Program
Lesson 13

How many sentences can you make? Procedure, Teacher's Manual page 99
(Student Workbook page72.) (Use separate lined paper for this exercise)
This is a new open ended exercise in lesson 13. It takes advantage of the growing skills of the learner and provides opportunity for creativity and greater expansion of concepts.

Directions: on this page is a number of words. See how many sentences you can make from these words. You may use any word more than once.

GLASS, LAD, FULL, LAST, SAM, FAST, HAD, DUG, A, GLAD, FALL, JUST, AND, HAS, NAN, TALL

Directions: Here is a list of words. your job is to make as many sentences as you can. you may use any word several times.

Special Review Lesson 13
Letters: G and H

Words: JAM HAM, JUG HUG, JUT HUT, JUG JAG, JUST GUST, JAG GAG.

Phrases and Sentences: AN ANT SAT AT A JAM JAR. JAN DUSTS A JUG. A RAT JUST HAD A JAM TART. A HARD JUT HURT SAM=S JAW. A RAT SAT AT A JAM JAR. SAM SAW A JAM JAR.

PICTURE PHRASES

DAN HAS JAM AND HAM

AN ANT AND A JAM JAR

LESSON 14 THE Letter/sound /L/

Purpose. Unit XV introduces THE Letter/sound /L/ as in LAST and related words. Included are words with a double L. The learner=s word and sentence synthesis processing and comprehension of words in sentences and phrases is again a major goal.

Timing Note: This lesson should take at least THREE sessions preferably separated by s whole day the. Teachers should judge by the quality of the learner=s responses whether to continue on or to rehearse for a longer period. Resting time between learning sessions for consolidation of learning is essential. Remember to start each session with a Review. Time is not important, Quality is.

Letter/sound: /L/ as in LAST. /L/ is formed by placing the tip of the tongue behind the upper teeth and allowing the sound to come around the sides of the tongue. Vibration of the vocal chords accompanies this passage of air.

Letter formation L
>L= the capital letter >L= is made from two lines

1. The first stroke is a vertical line from the top to the bottom of the letter.

2. The second line starts at the base of thevertical line and proceeds to the left. this l ine is less than half the length of the vertical line.

Words: ALAS, ALUM, DULL, GULL, GLAD, GLASS, LADS, LAG, LAND, LARD, LASS, LAST, LUG, LUST, SALAD, SLAG, SLAM, WALL, SLUG, SLUM, SLUR.

Comments. Up to LESSON 15, the games have emphasized working out the words. At this point most of the learners should be able to blend sounds into a slow transition through the tasks required for word recognition activities. We begin basing the games on speed to a greater and greater extent. The games in which speed is emphasized should be concerned largely with review materials.

Surprise Game. A card is placed face down on a card holder. A learner may have a turn to take a surprise. If he knows the surprise he may keep it. If not, he must put it back.

Professor Bloomer's No-Nonsense Reading Program
Lesson 14

L

PICTURES TO LABEL

SALAD

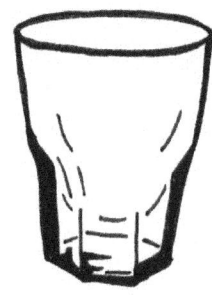
GLASS

FALL

FLAG

TALL HAT

HALL

HULL

Professor Bloomer's No-Nonsense Reading Program
Lesson 14

Beginning Review: Procedure, Teachers manual Page 6-7:
   (Use separate lined paper for this exercise)

   Letter/sounds /A/ /T/ /S/. /M/ /R/ /G/./F/, /W/, /R/ /N/ /U/, /H/ /J/
   and the words JAM, JAN, JAR, JAW, JUST, JUT, HAND, HARD, HARM,

Introducing the Letter/sound /L/, Procedure: Teacher's Manual page 1;

   (Student Workbook page 74)

The Letter/sound /L/ as in LAD i

Constructive Synthesis: Procedure: Teacher's Manual page 8;
   (Use separate lined paper for this exercise)

   ALAS, ALUM, DULL, GULL, GLAD, GLASS, LADS, LAG, LAND, LARD, LASS,
   LAST, LUG, LUST, SALAD, SLAG, SLAM, WALL, SLUG, SLUM, SLUR.

Pictures to Label: Procedure Teacher's Manual page 10: **(Student Workbook page 74)**
   GLASS, SALAD, FALL, FLAG, HALL, TALL HAT, HULL

Match and Label: Procedure, Teacher's Manual page 21: **(Student Workbook page 75)**
   . FLAG, LUG, RUG, JUG, FALL, LAND, HULL, SALT, GULL, SALAD, GLASS

Matching words: Procedure, Teacher's Manual page 16: **(Student Workbook page 76)**

LARD	GLASS
GLASS	DULL
LAD	LAND
SLAM	LAD
DULL	SLAM
LUG	LARD
LAND	GLAD
GLAD	LUG

Professor Bloomer's No-Nonsende Reading Program
Lesson 14s

MATCH AND LABEL

FLAG
LUGS
RUG
JUG
FALL
HULL
SALT
GULL
SALAD
GLASS
LAND

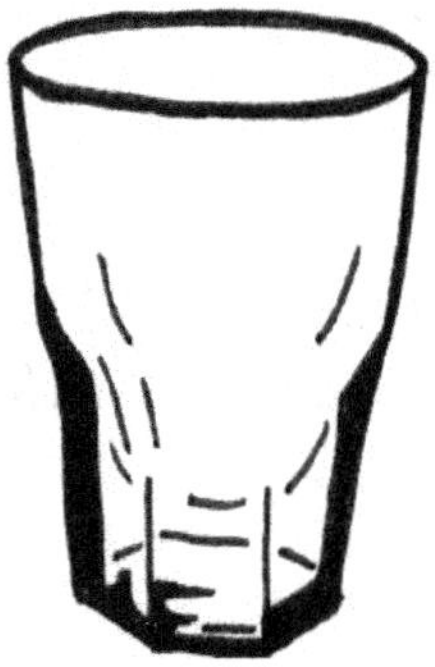

GLASS

FALL

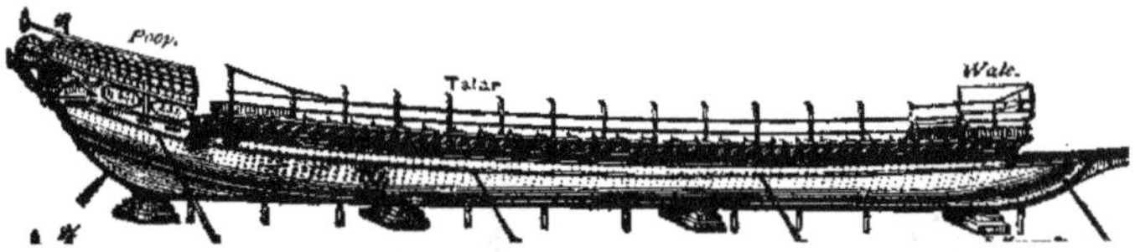

HULL

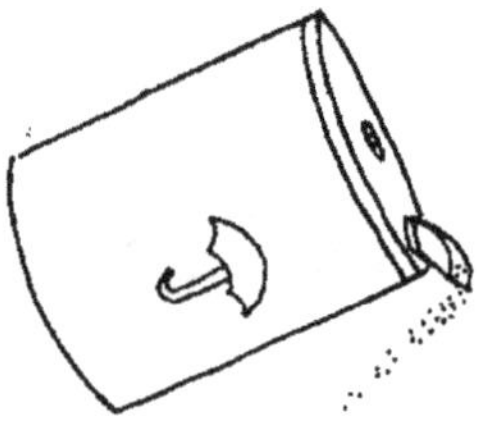

SALT

LUGS

LAND

GULL

SALAD

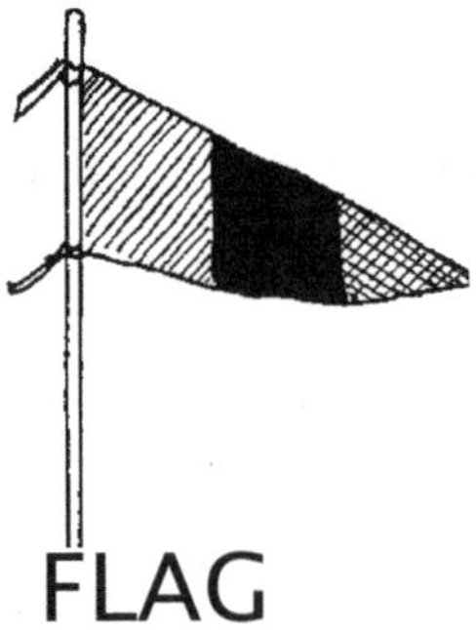

FLAG

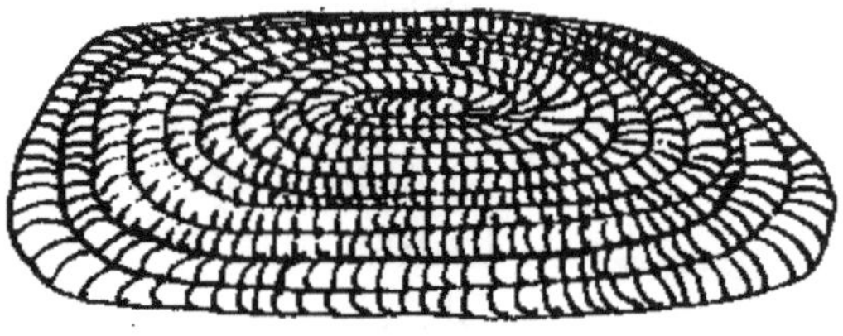

RUG

JUG

106

Professor Bloomer's No-Nonsensde Reading Program
Lesson 14

Finding word pairs and Reading Aloud: Procedure, Teacher's Manual page 16: **(Student Workbook page 76)** .

GLASS	LAST	**GLASS**	LAG
LAST	**LAD**	**LAD**	**D**ULL
LARD	**LASS**	GLAD	**LASS**
GLAD	**GLAD**	LAG	LAND
GLASS	**ALAS**	**ALAS**	LAW
SLAM	LAG	LASS	**SLAM**
LAND	GLAD	**LAG**	**LAG**
LAST	**LAST**	GLASS	LARD
LAG	**SALAD**	LAND	**SALAD**
DULL	LASS	**D**ULL	LARD
LAST	**GULL**	**GULL**	GLASS

Flash Identification: Procedure, Teacher's Manual page 46: **(Student Workbook page 77)** Expose the letters for two (2) seconds.

Letters to Flash are: **L, R, F, L, H, T, L, H.**

L	WA**LL**	WAR	**L**AD	HAD
R	HA**R**D	LAG	LA**R**D	**R**AG
F	**F**LAG	**F**AST	LAST	GLAD
L	HUM	TA**LL**	FU**LL**	DU**LL**
H	LAND	**H**AND	JAM	**H**ALL
T	LUG	GLASS	**T**UG	LASS
L	**F**LAT	TAG	LAG	SA**L**AD
H	**H**AD	LAW	JAW	**H**UG

Sounds in words: Procedure, Teacher's Manual page 32, **(Student Workbook page 77)** . The sequence of Letter/sounds to use in this lesson is as follow /L/, /U/, /H/, /U/, /T/, /M/, /G/, /S/.

/L/	HAM	A**L**AS	FAT	DU**L**L	FA**LL**
/U/	L**U**LL	SALAD	SLAT	TALL	L**U**G
/H/	SANTA	**H**ALL	**H**ULL	WALL	**H**AND
/U/	SL**U**G	GRASS	TAGGED	D**U**LL	LAST
/T/	**T**ALL	FLA**T**	JAM	HUM	FUR
/M/	GLASS	LAND	FLAG	SU**M**	NUT
/G/	SALAD	**G**ULL	**G**LAD	WALL	FALL
/S/	FLAG**S**	HULL	GLA**SS**	**S**LAT	LAD

10. WHAT IS THIS? CAN YOU MAKE IT BETTER?

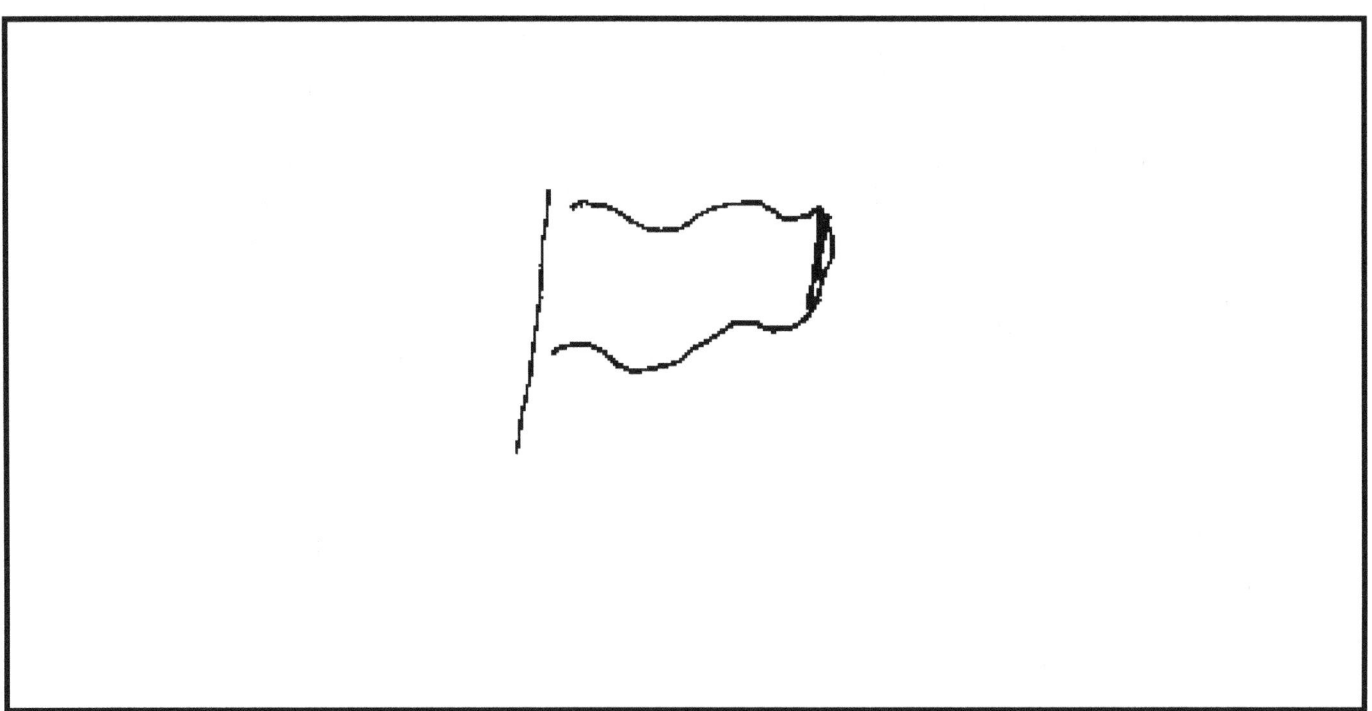

CAN YOU DRAW IT EVEN BETTER DOWN HERE?

Professor Bloomer's No-Nonsende Reading Program
Lesson 14

Dictation: Procedure, Teacher's Manual page 16: **(Student Workbook page 77)** **(Use separate lined paper for this exercise)**

Letter/soundS, /A/ /T/ /S/. /M/ /R/ /G/./F/, /W/, /R/ /N/ /U/, /H/ /J/, /L/
and the WORDS, ALAS, ALUM, DULL, GULL, GLAD, GLASS, LADS, LAG, LAND, LARD, LASS, LAST, LUG, LUST, SALAD, SLAG, SLAM, WALL, SLUG, SLUM, SLUR.

Picture completion: Procedure, Teacher's Manual page 46: **(Student Workbook page 78)**

How many words can you make? Procedure, Teacher's Manual page 32: **(Student Workbook page 79**

The Letter/sounds are. **L, R, A, F, U, M, T, S, G, H.**

Phrases to Read Aloud and Write: Procedure, Teacher's Manual page 37-38: **(Student Workbook page 79-80)** **(Use separate lined paper for this exercise)**

A LAD AND A LASS RAN FAST._____
A LAD HAD A SALAD AND WAS FULL. _____
NAN AND DAN HAD A FLAG. _____
A GLASS WALL WAS DULL._____
A FLAT RAFT HAD A TALL MAST._____
A TALL LAD DUG GRASS._____
A GULL TUGS AT A TART_____
MAMA AND DAD WERE GLAD._____
DAN WAS FULL ATLAST._____
A HUT HAD A FLAT WALL._____
LAND HAS MUD AND DUST._____

Completing Phrases: Procedure, Teacher's Manual page 38-39: **(Student Workbook page 80**

A FLAT RA**F**T HAD A TA**LL** MAST. (F, LL)
A **L**AD HAD A SA**L**AD. (L, L)
DAN RAN L**A**ST. (A)
A FARM HAD **H**ARD **L**AND. (H, L)
DAN HAD A FLA**G**. (G)

109

Professor Bloomer's No-Nonsense Reading Program
Lesson 14

Pictures to label: Procedure, Teacher's Manual page 38-39: **(Student Workbook page 81)**

GLASS. WALRUS, ANT HILL, FALL, A TALL MAN IN A TALL HAT

How many sentences can you make? Procedure, Teacher's Manual page 99: **(Student Workbook page 82) (Use separate lined paper for this exercise)**

GLASS, LAD, FULL, LAST, SAM, FAST, HAD, DUG, A, GLAD, FALL, JUST, AND, HAS, NAN, TALL **WAS, SAW, THE, A, AT. , WANTS** .

Special Review:
Letters. Review for sound: R Follow the procedure in lesson 8.

Review for shape: F, H, T, J. Follow the procedure in lesson 9

Words: Review for sound: RAG LAD, RUG LUG, FAD LAD, LUST LAST, TALL HALL, LULL FALL, MAST FLAT, JAM LAM, FALL FALSE, FLAG FLAT, HALL HULL, LAST TALL, SLAT STALL.

Phrases and sentences: A LAD AND A LASS RAN FAST. A LAD HAD A SALAD AND WAS FULL. NAN AND DAN HAD A FLAG. A GLASS WALL WAS DULL. A FLAT RAFT HAD A TALL MAST. A TALL LAD DUG GRASS. A MARE HAD A GRASS SALAD. A GULL TUGGED AT A TART. MAMA AND DAD WERE GLAD. DAN WAS FULL AT LAST. A HUT HAD A FLAT WALL. LAND HAS MUD AND DUST.

PICTURE PHRASES

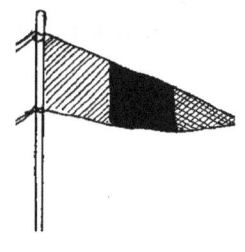

FLAG

WALRUS

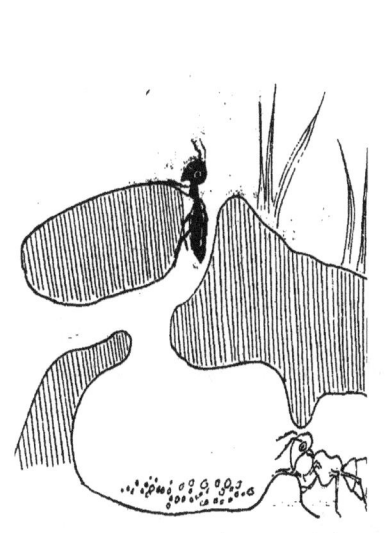

ANT HILL

FALL

FALL

A TALL MAN IN A TALL HAT

Professor Bloomer's No-Nonsense Reading Program
Lesson 15

Lesson 15 The Letter/sound /C/

Purpose. Lesson 15 introduces the Letter/sound /C/ as in CAT and related words. Children continue to grow in their understanding of the meanings of words and their relationship to one another.

Timing Note: This lesson should take at least FOUR sessions preferably separated by a whole day. Teachers should judge by the quality of the learner's responses whether to continue on or to rehearse for a longer period. Resting time between learning sessions for consolidation of learning is essential. Remember to start each session with a Review. Time is not important, Quality is.

Letter/sound /C/ The letter C has two sounds /K/ and /S/ the Letter/sound /K/ as in CAT is more common For initial teaching we will restrict ourselves to instances of the /K/ Letter/sound. /K/ is made by stopping a column of air with the middle of the tongue pressed against the roof of the mouth. The vocal chords do not vibrate. A voiced /K/ sounds /G/h.

Letter Formation **C**

'C' The capital letter 'C' is a single curved line.

1. The single stroke starts at 2 o'clock and curves to the left in a circular path around to five o'clock

Words. CAD, CALL, CAN, CANDLE, CAN'T, CAR, CARD, CAST, CAT, CAW, CRAM, CUD, CURD, CURT.

Beginning Review Procedure, Teachers manual Page 6-7: **(Use separate lined paper for this exercise)**
Letter/sounds /A/ /T/ /S/. /M/ /R/ /G/./F/, /W/, /R/ /N/ /U/, /H/ /J/, /L/
and the words, ALAS, ALUM, DULL, GULL, GLAD, GLASS, LADS, LAG, LAND, LARD, LASS, LAST, LUG, LUST, SALAD, SLAG, SLAM, WALL, SLUG, SLUM, SLUR.

Introducing the Letter/sound /C/, Procedure: Teacher's Manual page 1; **(Student Workbook page 83)** The Letter/sound /C/ as in CUT

Professor Bloomer's No-Nonsense Reading Program
Lesson 15

Constructive Synthesis: Procedure: Teacher's Manual page 8; **(Use separate lined paper for this exercise)**

    CAD, CALL, CAN, CANDLE, CAN'T, CAR, CARD, CART, CAST, CAT, CAW, CRAM, CUD, CURD, CURT SCAN.

Pictures to Label: Procedure Teacher's Manual page 10: **(Student Workbook page 83)**   CARDS CUT CAR CUFF CANDLE CLAM CAN, CARD, CARD.

Match and Label: Procedure, Teacher's Manual page 21: **(Student Workbook page 84)**   CAT, CAN, CARD, CAR, CRAG, DRAG, CART, CLAM

Matching words: Procedure, Teacher's Manual page 16: **(Student Workbook page 85)**

CAN	CAT
CAR	CAW
SCAN	CARD
CRAM	CRAM
CAT	CAR
CARD	SCAN
CAW	CRAFT
CRAFT	CAN

Finding word pairs and Reading Aloud : Procedure, Teacher's Manual page 16: **(Student Workbook page 85)**

CAN	**CAR**	LAND	**CAR**
SCAN	**SCAN**	CAN	CRAM
CAN	LARD	**CAN**	HAM
CALL	**CRAM**`	**CRAM**	SCRAM
CULL	CAR	CURD	**CULL**
CAD	**CUR**	**CUR**	CARD
SCAN	**CAW**	CALL	**CAW**
CARD	CUD	**CARD**	CRAM
CAR	**CAT**	**CAT**	SCAN
CURD	LAD	CALL	**CURD**

Professor Bloomer's No-Nonsense Reading Program
Lesson 15

C _____

_____

PICTURES TO LABEL

CARDS

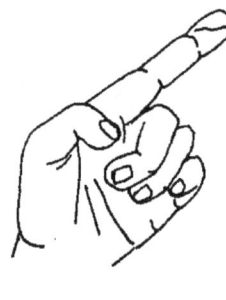
CUT

CAR

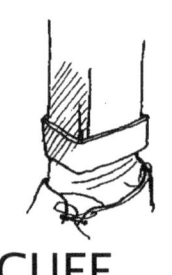
CUFF

CANDLE

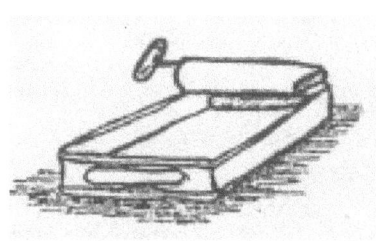
CAN

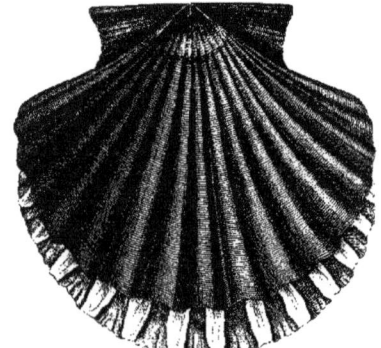
CLAM

CARD

CARD

114

MATCH AND LABEL

CAT
CAN
CARD
CAR
CRAG
DRAG
SCAN
CART
CLAM

CRAG

CAT

CAR

CARD

DRAG

CART

SCAN

CLAM

CUT

CAN

Professor Bloomer's No-Nonsense Reading Program
Lesson 15

Flash Identification: Procedure, Teacher's Manual page 46: **(Student Workbook page 86)**
Letters to Flash are: **C, G, T, C, D, L, U, C.**

C	**C**ART	GUST	DART	**C**RUST
G	CAT	CARD	CRA**G**	**G**AS
T	HAD	CAS**T**	CAR	**T**AR
C	GUST	DRAG`	A**C**T	**C**RAG
D	**D**AN	CALL	LAR**D**	GUST
L	FAST	CUR**L**	CAST	**L**AST
U	C**U**RD	CALL	C**U**RL	CRAG
C	**C**AT	**C**RAM	SAT	GAS

Sounds in words: Procedure, Teacher's Manual page 32: **(Student Workbook page 86)** Letter/sounds to be sounded: **C, R, C, L, D, N U, H.**

/C/	HAD	CRAM	DART	**C**UT	**C**ART
/R/	CA**R**	CU**R**D	LAST	DAN	D**R**UM
/C/	GIVE	RAG	**C**AST	**C**URT	FALL
/L/	CUR	**L**AD	HIS	CAT	S**L**AM
/D/	HA**D**	HULL	CAT	JAG	LAN**D**
/N/	SAT	HA**N**D	MI**N**T	CA**N**	CRAG
/U/	GLASS	SL**U**G	CR**U**ST	LAST	CAST
/H/	**H**ULL	CARD	**H**AS	MAST	DART

Dictation: Procedure, Teacher's Manual page 16: **(Student Workbook page 86)** **(Use separate lined paper for this exercise)**

Letter/soundS /A/ /T/ /S/. /M/ /R/ /G/./F/, /W/, /R/ /N/ /U/, /H/ /J/, /L/. /C/ and the WORDS, CAD, CALL, CAN, CANDLE, CAN'T, CAR, CARD, CART, CAST, CAT, CAW, CRAM, CUD, CURD, CURT SCAN.
Dictation should be presented in several sessions limited to lists of eight to ten Letter/sounds and words presented in random order.

Picture completion: Procedure, Teacher's Manual page 46: **(Student Workbook page 87)**

How many words can you make? Procedure, Teacher's Manual page 32: **(Student Workbook page 88)**
The Letters are **C, N, A, T, R, U, M, S, G**

Professor Bloomer's No-Nonsense Reading Program
Lesson 15

WHAT IS THIS?   CAN YOU MAKE IT BETTER?

CAN YOU DRAW IT BETTER DOWN HERE?

Professor Bloomer's No-Nonsense Reading Program
Lesson 15

Phrases to Read Aloud and Write Procedure, Teacher's Manual page 37-38, **(Student Workbook page 88)** **(Use separate lined paper for this exercise)**

A RAT CAN RUN. _____
A CAR CAN RUN FAST. _____
MAMA CALLS JAN. _____
DAN CRAMS A TART. _____
A CAR HAS GAS. _____
A CAT SAT ON A CRAG. _____
A RAT HAD A CRUST. _____
A CAT CAN HURT A RAT _____
DAN CAST A DART. _____
MAMA HAD A CARD. _____
SAM CAN DRAW A CAT. _____

Completing Phrases Procedure, Teacher's Manual page 38-39: **(Student Workbook page 89)**

DAN C_N'T CU_ A CAN. (A, T)
SAM CAN D_AW A C_T. (R, A)
A CAT CA_ HURT A RAT (N)
A CAT _AN R_N FAST. (C, U)
_N ANT CRAWLS AT A C_N. (A, A)
A CAT D_G MUD. (I)

Picture Phrases Procedure, Teacher's Manual page 21: **(Student Workbook page 89=90)**

CARDS, CACTUS, A CAT AND A HAT. CRAG (CASTLE) dAN DRAGS A CART.
A CAT AND A RAT. A CAR WANTS GAS. CATS.

How many sentences can you make? Procedure, Teacher's Manual page 99: **(Student Workbook page 90) (Use separate lined paper for this exercise)**

CAT, SAND, A, DUG, RUN, SAT, CAN, CALL, JAN, CAN'T, AND, CARD, SCAT, DAN, **WAS, SAW, THE, A, AT WANTS, HAD.**

` Pictures to label CARDS, CACTUS CAT AND A HAT, CAS-
TLE, DAN DRAGS A CART.   A CAT AND A RAT. CATS, CAR
AND GAS

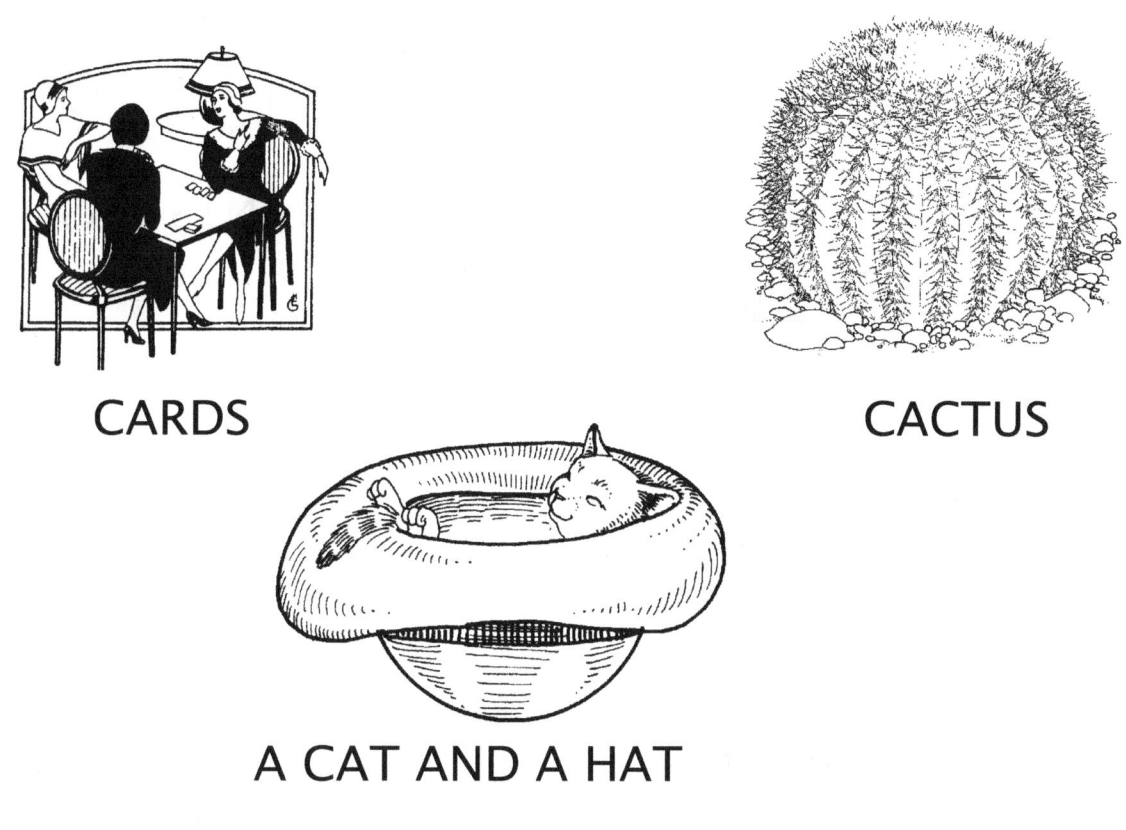

CARDS

CACTUS

A CAT AND A HAT

CRAG (CASTLE)

DAN DRAGS A CART

Professor Bloomer's No-Nonsensse Reading Program
Lesson 15

PICTURE PHRASES

A CAT AND A RAT

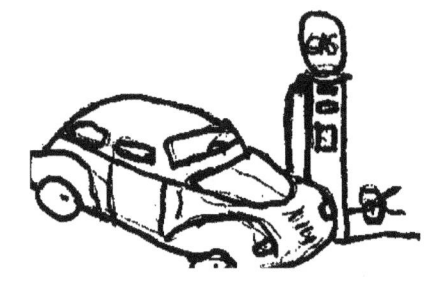

A CAR WANTS GAS

CATS

Special Review. Sound: Letters G T

Words: (CAT, TAT) (CAM, TAM) (CAR, TAR) (CRAM, TRAM) (CAT, GAT) (GUT, CUT) (CULL, GULL) (CAN, TAN) (ACT, CAN'T) (CAST, CART)

Shape: Letters D G

Words: (DAM, CAM) (DAN, CAN) (CULL, CURD) (CRAFT, DRAFT) (CRAG, DRAG) (CARE, DARE) (CRAM, DRAM) (CUB, DUB) (CARD, CURD) (CRUST, DUST)

Sentences and phrases: A CAT CAN HURT A RAT.   A CAR CAN RUN FAST. A GIRL CAN RINSE A JAR. MAMA WAS CURT. A CAR CAN RUST. A CUB SWAM. A CAT SAT ON A CRAG. A CAT AND A CUB HAD A CAN

Professor Bloomer's No-Nonsense Reading Program
Lesson 16

Lesson 16 The VOWEL Letter/sound /I/

Purpose: Lesson 16 introduces the Letter/sound /I/as in ILL and related words. The introduction of an additional vowel sound serves to increase the number of words available. The unit will be mostly concerned with increasing the child's comprehension of the new materials.

Timing Note: This lesson should take at least FIVE sessions preferably separated by a whole day. Teachers should judge by the quality of the learner's responses whether to continue on or to rehearse for a longer period. Resting time between learning sessions for consolidation of learning is essential. Remember to start each session with a Review. Time is not important, Quality is.

Letter/sound /I/ as in ILL is formed high in the front of the mouth. The lips are unrounded and are not tense. /I/ is voiced. The lips are less rounded than for /E/.

\Letters formation: I
'I' the capital letter

   1. 'I' is a single vertical stroke from the top to the bottom of the letter

Words:. DID, DIG, DIM, DIN, FIG, FILL, FIN, FIST, HID, GIG, GILL, GIRL, FIRM, IF, IN, IS, JILL, JIM, MID, MISS, RID, RIG, SILL, SIS, SWIM, WIG, WIN, WIND. WILL

  Beginning Review: Procedure, Teachers manual Page 6-7: **(Use separate lined paper for this exercise)**

     Letter/sounds /A/ /T/ /S/. /M/ /R/ /G/./F/, /W/, /R/ /N/ /U/, /H/ /J/, /L/. /C/
    and the words, **CAD, CALL, CAN, CANDLE, CAN'T, CAR, CARD, CART, CAST, CAT, CAW, CRAM, CUD, CURD, CURT SCAN.**

Introducing the Letter/sound /I/, Procedure: Teacher's Manual page 1; **(Student Workbook page 91)**
The Letter/sound /I/ as in IT i

Professor Bloomer's No-Nonsense Reading Program
Lesson 16

I_____

_____

PICTURES TO LABEL

MILL

WIND

FIN

GIRL

HID

MITT

GIFT

Professor Bloomer's No-Nonsense Reading Program
Lesson 16

Constructive Synthesis: Procedure: Teacher's Manual page 8; **(Use separate lined paper for this exercise)**

    DID, DIG, DIM, DIN, FIG, FILL, FIN, FIST, HID, GIG, GILL, GIRL, FIRM, IF, IN, IS, JILL, JIM, MID, MISS, RID, RIG, , SILL, SIS, SWIM, WIG, WIN, WIND. WILL.

Pictures to Label: Procedure Teacher's Manual page 10: **(Student Workbook page 91)**
    MILL, WIND, ILL, FIN, HID, GIFT

Match and Label: Procedure, Teacher's Manual page 21: **(Student Workbook page 92)** Follow the procedure in lesson 3

    MILL, MISS, HIT, MIT, GIRL, SING, FIG, FIN, GIFT, LID

Matching Words: Procedure, Teacher's Manual page 16: **(Student Workbook page 93)**

SING	SWIM
WIN	DIM
RISK	MISS
FIRM	IS
DIG	WIN
DIM	FIRM
IS	DIG
MISS	RISK
SWIM	SING

Finding word pairs and Reading Aloud: Procedure, Teacher's Manual page 16: **(Student Workbook page 93)**

FIRM	**SWIM**	WIN	**SWIM**
IF	FIN	JIM	**IF**
IS	**SIS**	**SIS**	RINSE
DID	**DID**	FIG	WIN
LID	MISS	**GIVE**	**GIVE**
RINSE	**FIN**	**FIN**	TAR
IN	JIG	**IN**	JIM
RIM	**FIG**	**FIG**	CARD
DID	**IS**	**IS**	SAT
JIM	CURT	**JIM**	DIM
FIRM	**FIRM**	FIG	FIST

Professor Bloomer's No-Nonsense Reading Program
Lesson 16

MATCH AND LABEL

MILL
MISS
HIT
MIT
GIRL
SING
FIG
FIN
GIFT
LID

GIRL

MILL

MITT

FIG

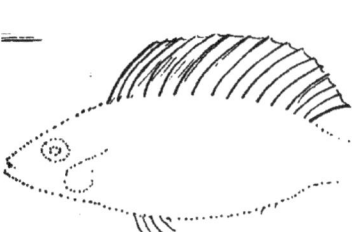
FIN

HIT

LID

SING

GIFT

MISS

Professor Bloomer's No-Nonsense Reading Program
Lesson 16

Flash Identification: Procedure, Teacher's Manual page 46: **(Student Workbook page 94)** Expose the letters for two (2) seconds
Letters to Flash are: I, A, H, I, L, I, T, I.

i	DAD	DID	LAD	AM**I**D
A	S**A**T	IN	DIRT	SL**A**M
H	FIT	**H**ID	HIT	SIT
I	L**I**TTLE	F**I**N	FAN	FLAT
L	HID	HI**LL**	**L**AD	FA**LL**
I	H**I**LL	DIRT	DART	HALT
T	GIF**T**	ILL	**T**IN	DAN
I	HAS	H**I**S	LAST	L**I**ST

Sounds in words: Procedure, Teacher's Manual page 32: **(Student Workbook page 94)**
Sounds in words. /I/, /T/, /L/, /W/, /J/, /D/, /F/, /S/.

/I/	G**I**G	CAST	L**I**MIT	SLAT	H**I**LL
/T/	RIM	FI**T**	LIS**T**	FAN	MIS**T**
/L/	**L**ARD	DARE	MI**LL**	HIM	**L**IST
/W/	VAST	**W**IG	HAD	S**W**AM	S**W**IM
/J/	SLIM	TRIM	**J**IM	RIG	**J**AW
/D/	**D**IM	**D**RAM	FIST	RAFT	TIM
/F/	**F**IG	MISS	LID	**F**IN	GI**F**T
/S/	I**S**	**S**AT	JIM	CAR**S**	DIM

Dictation Procedure, Teacher's Manual page 16: **(Student Workbook page 94)**
(Use separate lined paper for this exercise)

Letter/sound**S** /A/ /T/ /S/. /M/ /R/ /G/./F/, /W/, /R/ /N/ /U/, /H/ /J/, /L/. /C/, /I/ and the WORDS, DID, DIG, DIM, DIN, FIG, FILL, FIN, FIST, HID, GIG, GILL, GIRL, FIRM, IF, IN, IS, JILL, JIM, MID, MISS, RID, RIG, RISE, SILL, SIS, SWIM, WIG, WIN, WIND, WILL.

How many words can you make? (Student Workbook page 96)
The Letter/sounds are **I, W, M, S, R, T, L, N, D, A.**

Professor Bloomer's No-Nonsense Reading Program
Lesson 16

WHAT IS THIS? CAN YOU MAKE IT BETTER?

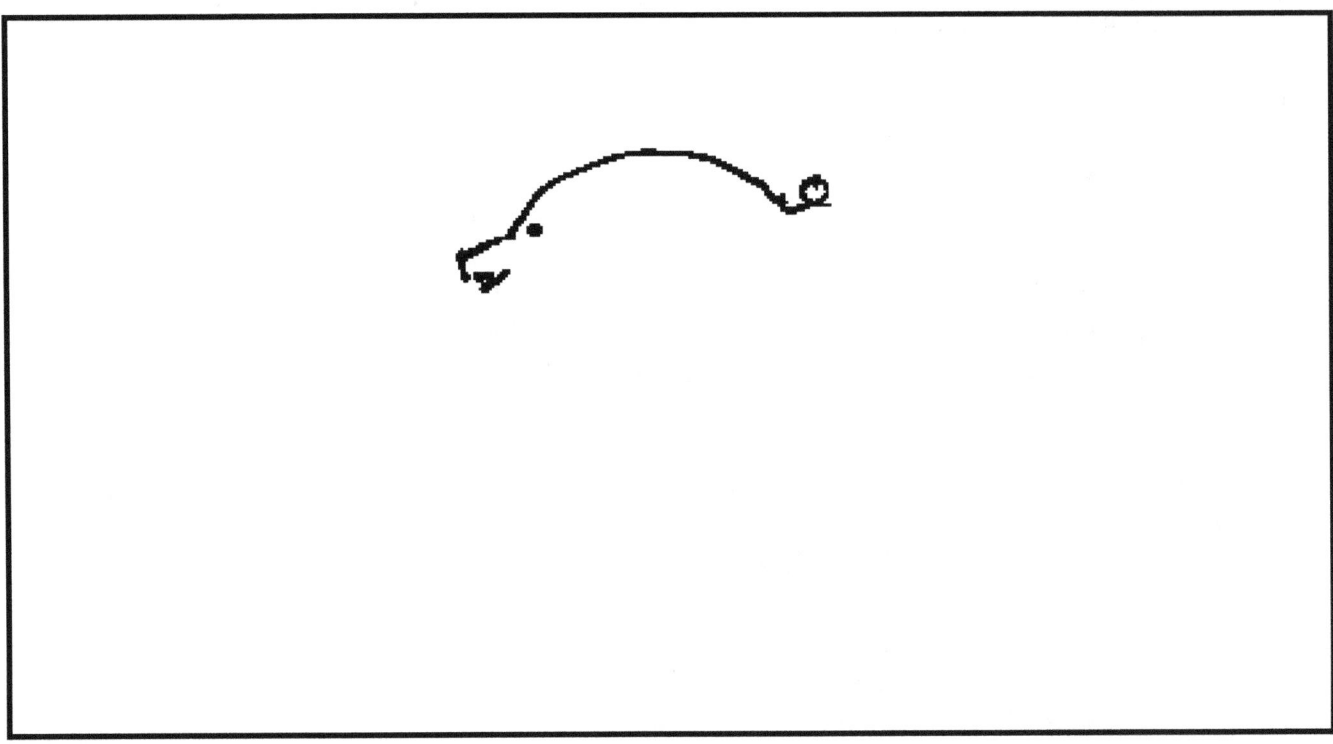

CAN YOU DRAW IT BETTER DOWN HERE?

Professor Bloomer's No-Nonsense Reading Program
Lesson 16

Picture completion: Procedure, Teacher's Manual page 46: **(Student Workbook page 95)**

Phrases to Read Aloud and Write Procedure, Teacher's Manual page 37-38: **(Student Workbook page 96) (Use separate lined paper for this exercise)**

A RAT RAN IN A MILL._____
AN ANT WAS IN A SAND HILL._____
AN ANT WAS IN A SALAD._____
JILL IS A GIRL._____
JILL WILL RINSE A JAR. IN A SINK_____
JILL MUST RUN A HILL._____
A MIST HID A HILL._____
JILL WILL WIN AT TAG._____
JIM WILL GIVE TIM A WIG._____
A MAN'S HAT MUST FIT_____

Completing Phrases: Procedure, Teacher's Manual page 38-39 **(Student Workbook page 97)**

J_M AND SIS H_D A GIFT. (I, A),
TIM W_LL VISIT SAM. (I,)
A _AN'S HAT MUST F_T. (M, I,)
A CAN _S T_N. (I,I)
DAN WAS ILL IN A W_RD.(A)
A RAT CAN R_N _N A M_LL. (U, I)
A CAT CAN D__G IN SAND. (I)
__N ANT SAT __N A JAM J__R LID. (A, I, A)

Pictures Phrases to Label: Procedure, Teacher's Manual page 21: **(Student Workbook page 97-98)**
DAN AND JILL HAVE A GIFT. A CANDLE IS LIT. FILL A CAN. A SWIFT, SNIPS, WIND, GRIFFIN, TUG, JIG, HUNT, HUG, IN, INN

How many sentences can you make? Procedure, Teacher's Manual page 99: **(Student Workbook page 98) (Use separate lined paper for this exercise)**

CAN, MAN, MILL, ANT, HURT, HAD, HAT, HAS, GULL, DIRT, HULL, HIS, FIR, AN, SIS, SWIM, AND, NAN, JUST, RAN. **UNDER, WAS, SAW, THE, A, UP, AT IT, IS, IN WANTS.**

Professor Bloomer's No-Nonsense Reading Program
Lesson 16

Comments. /I/ is one of the more difficult vowel sounds and thus the children should have it's sound well learned before the Special sound review is begun. A large number of words are available for this purpose. Work on all of them. With the great increase in the number of words the teacher should be sure that the meanings of all the words are clear to the children.

Special Review:
Sound: Letters: A H

Words: (AT, IT) (SAT, SIT) (TIM, TAM) (MISS, MASS) (RIM, RAM) (RIG, RAG) (GIG, GAG) (FIT, FAT) (FIST, FAST) (WIG, WAG) (DIM, DAM) (MID, MAD) (DIRT, DART) (DID) DAD) JIM (TIN, TAN) (FIN, FAN) (DIN, DAN) (MIST, MAST) (HIT, HAT) (HIM, HAM) (HIS, HAS) (HID, HAD) (LID, LAD) (LIST, LAST) (WILL, WALL) (FILL, FALL) (HILL, HALL) (JIG, JOG) AMID, HILT, HILL, FILL, LATIN, LIMIT, LIST, LIT, LITTLE, SLIT DRIFT, SIFT HID, HIM, HIS FIT SLIM, JILT, JINGLE TWIG, IF MILL, MIDDLE DIRT, MIST, ILL, SLIM, FIST, MINT. RILL, WILL, GIFT, MITT, SILL, ILL SATIN, SIT, TIN, TEN, TRIM

Shape: Letters H L T
Words: (HIT, HAT) (HIM, HAM) (HIS, HAS) (HID, HAD) (LID, LAD) (LIST, LAST) TIM (FIST, FIT) (LIT, NIT, HIT) (FILL, HILL) (LITTLE, LIMIT) LIVE, SLIM, VISIT

Sentences and phrases:
DAN HID IN A BAG. A RAFT WAS IN MUD. A JAR HAD A LID. NAN WILL STIR A SALAD. A VAT WILL FILL A JUG. JIM WILL GIVE TIM A WIG. JIM IS IN A FIT. A RIM WILL SINK IN MUD. JILL WILL WIN AT TAG. DAN CAN TRIM A RAM. JIM IS A WIT. A CAR CAN'T RUN IN THE MUD. DAN CAN RINSE A JAR. JILL CAN GIVE SAM A TART. A CUB CAN DIG IN MUD AND DUST. DAN CUT A LITTLE SLIT. A CUB DID A JIG. A CAT HISSED AT A CUR. A CAN IS TIN. A CUB CAN HAVE FUN IN MUD. A RAT CAN DO A JIG. JILL CAN GIVE SAM A TART. A CAT CAN DIG IN MUD. A CAT CAN SWIM. A CAN IS TIN. A GIRL CAN HAVE A DUST RAG. SAM HAS A STIFF HAND. A RAT RAN IN A MILL. AN ANT WILL SIT IN A SAND HILL. DAN HID IN A MIST. DAN SWIMS IN A RIVER. DAN WAS ILL IN A WARD. JIM CAN'T SWIM. DAN CUT A LITTLE SLIT IN A MAT. IF A RAT CAN RUN, A RAT HAS FUN. A RAT SAT IN A JAM JAR LID. SAM WILL WIN IT. A CANDLE WAS LIT. JILL IS A GIRL.

PICTURE PHRASES

DAN AND NAN HAD A GIFT

FILL A CAN

SWIFT

WIND

A CANDLE IS LIT   GRIFFIN

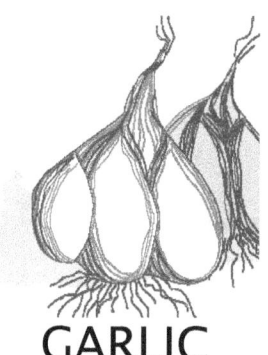
GARLIC

HUG

TUG JIG HUNT

HUG IN INN

HOW MANY SENTENCES CAN YOU MAKE

CAN	MAN	MILL	ANT	HURT	HAD	HAT
HAS	GULL	DIRT	IN	HULL	HIS	FIT
AN	SWIM	A	NAN	JUST	RAN	AND

Lesson 17 The Letter/sound /V/

Purpose: Unit 18 introduces the Letter/sound V as in VAT and related words. The emphasis of this unit should be on consolidating the material thus far presented in mechanics and understanding.

Timing Note: This lesson should take at least THREE sessions preferably separated by a whole day. Teachers should judge by the quality of the learner's responses whether to continue on or to rehearse for a longer period. Resting time between learning sessions for consolidation of learning is essential. Remember to start each session with a Review. Time is not important, Quality is.

Letter/sound /V/ : /V/ as in VAT is formed by placing the upper front teeth close to the lower lip and forming a column of air between them. This is accompanied by a vibration of the vocal chords. /V/ which is not voiced sounds /F/.

Letter formation: V

'V' The capital letter 'V' is made with two straight lines

1. The first stroke starts at the top of the letter and angles down to the right at about 600
2. The second stroke starts at the top of thee letter, a letters width to the right and angles down to the left at about 600 to meet the first stroke at the bottom of the letter.

Words: HAVE, LAVA, VAN, VAST, VAT, VISIT, GIVE, VULTURE

Beginning Review: Procedure, Teachers manual Page 6-7: **(Use separate lined paper for this exercise)**
Letter/sounds /A/ /T/ /S/. /M/ /R/ /G/./F/, /W/, /R/ /N/ /U/, /H/ /J/, /L/. /C/, /I/. and the words, DID, DIG, DIM, DIN, FIG, FILL, FIN, FIST, HID, GIG, GILL, GIRL, FIRM, IF, IN, IS, JILL, JIM, MID, MISS, RID, RIG, RISE, SILL, SIS, SWIM, WIG, WIN, WIND. WILL

Introducing the Letter/sound /V/, Procedure: Teacher's Manual page 1; **(Student Workbook page 99)**

The Letter/sound /V/ as in VAN

Professor Bloomer's No-Nonsense Reading Program
Lesson 17

V_____

PICTURES TO LABEL

VAN

GIVE (A GIFT)

LAVA

VISIT

VĀN

VAST (LAND)

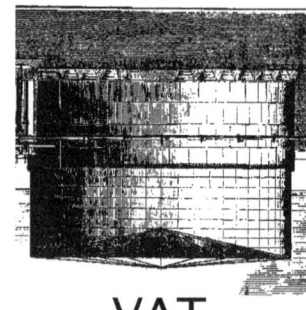
VAT

Professor Bloomer's No-Nonsense Reading Program
Lesson 17

Constructive Synthesis: Procedure: Teacher's Manual page 8; **(Use separate lined paper for this exercise)**

    HAVE, LAVA, VAN, VAST, VAT, VISIT, GIVE.

Pictures to Label: Procedure Teacher's Manual page 10: **(Student Workbook page 99)**

    VAN, VISIT, GIVE, LAVA, VAT, VAN, LAVA or VAST,

Match and Label: Procedure, Teacher's Manual page 21: **(Student Workbook page 100)**

    VAT, MAT, LAVA, VISIT, MAN, VAST, MAST, LIST, FIST, FAN, SWIM.

Matching words: Procedure, Teacher's Manual page 16: **(Student Workbook page 101)**

VISIT	LAVA
HAVE	VAN
LAVA	VAST
VISTA	VAT
VAT	VISIT
VAST	VISTA
VAN	HAVE

Finding word Pairs and Reading Aloud: Procedure, Teacher's Manual page 16: **(Student Workbook page 101**

HAVE	**HAVE**	VISIT	VAT
VISTA	**LAVA**	VAST	**LAVA**
HAVE	**VAST**	**VAST**	VIST
VISTA	LAVA	VISIT	**VISTA**
VAST	**VAT**	HAVE	**VAT**
LAVA	VAT	**VISIT**	**VISIT**
VAN	VISIT	**VAN**	VISTA

133

MATCH AND LABEL

VAT
MAT
LAVA
VISIT
VAN
MAN
VAST
MAST
LIST
FIST
FAN
SWIM

LAVA

VAT

MAN

MAST (WIND)

VISIT

VAN

VAST, (CACTUS, SUN)

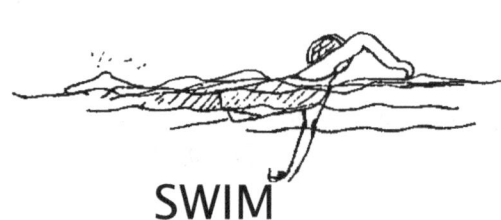

SWIM

LIST

MAT

FIST

Professor Bloomer's No-Nonsense Reading Program
Lesson 17

Flash Identification. Procedure, Teacher's Manual page 46: **(Student Workbook page 101)**
Letters to Flash are: **V, F, A, V, N, W, M, V.**

V	HA**V**E	MAT	**V**AST	**V**ISIT
F	VAST	**F**AT	VAT	**F**IRST
A	V**A**ST	MIST	M**A**ST	VISIT
V	FARM	WAS	CAT	**V**AST
N	LAVA	VAT	HAD	**N**AT
W	SA**W**	RAM	VAN	RA**W**
M	WAR**M**	VAN	**M**AN	NAT
V	**V**AST	MAST	**V**AT	WAS

Sounds in words: Procedure, Teacher's Manual page 32: **(Student Workbook page 102)**
The sequence of Letter/sounds to use in this lesson is as follows   /V/, /L/, /N/, /U/, /V/, /S/, /L/. /I/

/N/	SLAT	LAVA	HARM	**N**AT	LUG
/L/	MUST	DRUM	F**L**AT	**L**AVA	HARM
/N/	DUB	SWA**N**	SUM	FLAG	VA**N**
/U/	HARE	GLASS	HAVE	SW**U**M	**U**S
/V/	**V**AN	SLAG	LAST	**V**AST	MUST
/S/	LAVA	VA**S**T	ALUM	**S**WAM	LARD
/L/	ALUM	SLAM	DRAG	**L**AVA	HARD
/I/	VIS**I**T	SW**I**M	LAVA	SWUM	D**I**M

Dictation: Procedure, Teacher's Manual page 16: **(Student Workbook page 102) (Use separate lined paper for this exercise)**

Letter/sounds /A/, /T,/ /S/, /M/, /R/, /G/, /F/, /W/, /R/ /N/ /U/, /H/ /J/, /L/, /C/, /I/, /V/, and the WORDS, HAVE, LAVA, VAN, VAST, VAT, VISIT, GIVE VISTA.

How many words can you make? Procedure, Teacher's Manual page 32: **(Student Workbook page 192)**

The letters are **V, L, A, H. I. S. T. N. R,,U.**

Professor Bloomer's No-Nonsense Reading Program
Lesson 17

WHAT IS THIS?   CAN YOU MAKE IT BETTER?

CAN YOU DRAW IT BETTER DOWN HERE?

Professor Bloomer's No-Nonsense Reading Program
Lesson 17

Picture completion: Procedure, Teacher's Manual page 46: **(Student Workbook page 103)**

Phrases to Read Aloud and Write: Procedure, Teacher's Manual page 37-38: **(Student Workbook page 104) (Use separate lined paper for this exercise)**

```
TIM AND SIS HAVE A GIFT._____
MAMA AND DAD HAVE A FLAG._____
A VAST LAND WAS DUST AND SAND._____
RATS AND CATS HAVE FUN._____
A FULL VAN HAD A FLAT._____
A VAT WILL FILL A JUG._____
IF DAN CALLS TIM WILL VISIT HIM._____
MAMA AND DAD HAVE A VAN_____
SAM IS IN A VAT._____
```


Completing Phrases: Procedure, Teacher's Manual page 38-39: **(Student Workbook page 104)**

```
A   VAN   SAN__   IN   THE   MUD. (K)
A   __AN'S   HAT   MUST   __IT. (M, F)
MACK   HAS   A   HAR__   TASK. (D)
NAN   WILL   ASK   SANTA   __OR   A   GI__T. (F, F)
A   CAT   _AN   SWI_. (C, M)
A   FULL   _AN   HAD   A   FLAT. (V)
SAM   H_D   IN   A   _AT. (I, V)
TIM   W__LL   VIS_T   SAM. (I, I)
```

Pictures Phrases: Procedure, Teacher's Manual page 21: **(Student Workbook page 105)**
VULTURE, VAT, VAN, VAN, SAM RAN AT A VAT. SAM HID IN A VAT

How many sentences can you make? Procedure, Teacher's Manual page 99: **(Student Workbook page 106) (Use separate lined paper for this exercise)**

CAT, AND, CAN, WANTS, TIN, SAM, VAT, RAT, VAN, FUN, VISIT, RUN, SWIM, NAN, VISTA, SAW, HAVE, **UNDER, WAS, THE, A, UP, AT IT, IS, IN.**

Special Review:
    Sound—Letters F

    Words—(VAT, FAT) (VAN, FAN) (VAST, FAST)

    Shape—Letters A, M, N, W

    Words—(MAT, VAT) (NAT, VAT) (MAN, VAN) (NAN, VAN) (MAST, VAST)

Sentences and Phrases: A VAT WAS FULL. MAMA AND DAD HAVE A FLAG. A VAST LAND WAS DUST. A VAT HAD HAM AND LARD. RATS HAVE FUN. A VAN MUST HAVE A WALL. FAT RATS HAVE TAN FUR. A MAN MUST HAVE A LAND.

PICTURE PHRASES

VULTURE

VAT

VAN

VAN

DAN RAN AND HID IN A VAT

Professor Bloomer's No-Nonsense Reading Program
Lesson 18

Lesson 18 The Letter/sound /K/

Purpose: Lesson 18 introduces the Letter/sound K as in KICK and related words. Emphasis is placed on the similarity of sound between C and K. The meanings of the new words and the comprehension of the words in context is stressed.

Timing Note: This lesson should take at least FOUR sessions preferably separated by a whole day. Teachers should judge by the quality of the learner's responses whether to continue on or to rehearse for a longer period. Resting time between learning sessions for consolidation of learning is essential. Remember to start each session with a Review. Time is not important, Quality is.

Letter/sound /K/: K/ as in KICK is made by stopping a column of air with the middle of the tongue pressed against the roof of the mouth. The vocal chords do not vibrate. A voiced /K/ sounds /G/.

Letter formation:
'K' The capital letter 'K' is made from three lines

1. The first stroke is a vertical line from the top to the bottom of the letter.

2. The second stroke begins in the middle of the first line and proceeds upward and to the right at 45 degrees.

3. The third stroke begins in the middle of the first line and proceeds downward and to the right at 45 degrees.

Words: KID, KILL, KIM, KIN, KINK, KISS, ASK, DARK, JUNK, INK, KIT, LARK, MARK, MASK, RINK, SKULL, SKILL, DRINK, DRANK, LURK, MARK, MILK, MINK, MURK, RANK, RINK, RISK, SANK, SILK, SKAT, SKID, SKIM, SKIN, SKIT, SUNK, TANK, TASK, TURK, TUSK, WINK, WALK, SALT.

NOTE: Care should be taken to show the children that C and K have the same sound.

Beginning Review Procedure, Teachers manual Page 6-7: **(Use separate lined paper for this exercise)**

Letter/sounds /A/ /T/ /S/. /M/ /R/ /G/./F/, /W/, /R/ /N/ /U/, /H/ /J/, /L/. /C/, /I/ /V/.
and the words, HAVE, LAVA, VAN, VAST, VAT, VISIT, GIVE, VISTA.

The Letter/sound /K/, Procedure: Teacher's Manual page 1;**(Student Workbook page 107)** The letter/sound /K/ as in KICK

Professor Bloomer's No-Nonsense Reading Program
Lesson 18

K _____

_____

PICTURES TO LABEL

CLOCK

MILK

DUCKS

INK

VATS

KICK

SKUNK

DOCK

Professor Bloomer's No-Nonsense Reading Program
Lesson 18

Constructive Synthesis: Procedure: Teacher's Manual page 8; **(Use separate lined paper for this exercise)**

KID, KILL, KIM, KIN, KINK, KISS, ASK, DARK, JUNK, INK, KIT, LARK, MARK, MASK RINK, SKULL, SKILL, DRINK, DRANK, LURK, MARK, MILK, MINK, MURK, RANK, RINK, RISK, SANK, SILK, SKID, SKIM, SKIN, SKIT, SUNK, TANK, TASK, TURK, TUSK, WINK, WALK, SALT.

Begin this exercise by having yoiur learner reading these words aloud. Use Constructive Synthesis for words he has trouble with.

Pictures to Label: Procedure Teacher's Manual page 10: **(Student Workbook page 107)**

CLOCK, DUCKS MILK, INK, VATS, KICK, SKUNK.

Match and Label: Procedure, Teacher's Manual page 21: **(Student Workbook page 108)**

SKIRT, SINK, INK, HIT, DUCKS, KICK, TACK, TRUNK, MILK, WALK, SACK.

Matching words: Procedure, Teacher's Manual page 16, **(Student Workbook page 109)**

INK	JUNK
JACK	ASK
ASK	JACK
TUCK	DICK
DARK	INK
DICK	DARK
JUNK	LICK
LICK	TUCK

Finding word pairs and Reading Aloud: Procedure, Teacher's Manual page 16, **(Student Workbook page 109)**.

WINK	ASK	DICK	**WINK**
CLACK	**TACK**	DARK	**TACK**
RANK	DICK	**RANK**	SINK
SKID	**SLACK**	INK	**SLACK**
TANK	**TANK**	RANK	RISK
ASK	**SACK**	**SACK**	DUST
TUCK	SAND	**SANK**	**SANK**
LICK	**DUCK**	**DUCK**	MARK
MASK	SKID	MUSK	**MASK**
SILK	MUSK	**SINK**	**SINK**

MATCH AND LABEL

SKIRT
SINK
INK
FIST
DUCKS
DOCK
KICK
TACK
TRUNK
MILK
WALK
SACK

INK

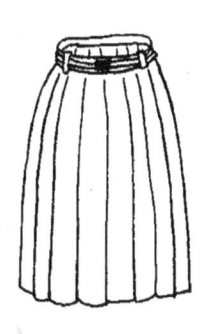
SKIRT

SACK

KICK

TACK

DUCKS

DOCK

TRUNK

FIST

SINK

MILK

WALK

Professor Bloomer's No-Nonsense Reading Program
Lesson 18

Flash Identification: Procedure, Teacher's Manual page 46 **(Student Workbook page 110**
Letters to Flash are: **K, V, F, H, K, R, K, H**.

K	HIC**K**	HID	**K**ID	FAT
V	LA**V**A	MAD	WAR	MAN
F	KIT	**F**IT	HIT	**F**IRST
H	MAD	**H**UNK	KIT	**H**IT
K	IN**K**	FIN	DRIN**K**	VAT
R	LA**R**K	**R**ID	**R**UG	KID
K	DRAG	FARM	DRIN**K**	HARD
H	DUSK	**H**IT	SKILL	**H**ILL

Sounds in words: Procedure, Teacher's Manual page 32: **(Student Workbook page 110)**

The sequence of Letter/sounds to use in this lesson is as follows:
/K/, /N/, /A/, /I/, /K/, /M/, /L/, /N/, /K/.

/K/	DUN**K**	DU**CK**	KI**CK**	HAT	JAM
/N/	KI**N**K	TACK	SACK	SI**N**K	KID
/A/	D**A**RK	**A**SK	SUNK	DR**A**NK	DICK
/I/	V**I**SIT	DUCK	**I**NK	STACK	LUCK
/K/	TU**CK**	DIG	JA**CK**	LI**CK**	LIT
/M/	**M**ASK	KISS	**M**ARK	RINK	**M**INT
/L/	DUSK	DRAG	**L**ARK	**L**INK	HUNK
/N/	KIT	HIT	I**N**K	FI**N**	DRI**N**K
/K/	VAT	LAR**K**	RID	RUG	**K**ID

Dictation: Procedure, Teacher's Manual page 16, **(Student Workbook page 110)**
(Use separate lined paper for this exercise)

Letter/soundS: /A/ /T/ /S/. /M/ /R/ /G/./F/, /W/, /R/ /N/ /U/, /H/ /J/, /L/. /C/, /I/ /V/. and the WORDS, KID, KILL, KIM, KIN, KINK, KISS, ASK, DARK, JUNK, INK, KIT, LARK, MARK, MASK, RINK, SKULL, SKILL, DRINK, DRANK, LURK, MARK, MILK, MINK, MURK, RANK, RINK, RISK, SANK, SILK, SKAT, SKID, SKIM, SKIN, SKIT, SUNK, TANK, TASK, TURK, TUSK, WINK, WALK, SALT.

Picture completion: Procedure, Teacher's Manual page 46: **(Student Workbook page 111)**

WHAT IS THIS? CAN YOU MAKE IT BETTER?

CAN YOU DRAW IT BETTER DOWN HERE?

Professor Bloomer's No-Nonsense Reading Program
Lesson 18

How many words can you make? Procedure, Teacher's Manual page 32: **(Student Workbook page 112)**
The letters are: K, D, C, I, U, R, N, S, L, G, A, V.

Phrases to Read Aloud and Write: Procedure, Teacher's Manual page 37-38: **(Student Workbook page 112) (Use separate lined paper for this exercise)**

IT IS DARK IN A SACK._____
DICK WILL KISS HIS MAMA._____
A DUCK CAN SWIM._____
JACK HAD A DARK MASK._____
JACK HAD A HARD TASK._____
SIS SAT ON A TACK._____
A CAT WILL LICK A KIT._____
A VAN SANK IN MUD._____
A SWAN WILL SWIM AT DUSK._____
AN ANT SWAM IN AN INK JAR._____
JACK FALLS, AND HURTS HIS SKULL._____
A CAT WILL DRINK MILK_____

Completing Phrases: Procedure, Teacher's Manual page 38-39: **(Student Workbook page 112)**

JACK HAD A DARK MAS**K**. (K)
DAN **H**AD A **H**ARD TAS**K**. (H, H, K)
JAN WILL AS**K** SANT**A**. (K, A)
A DU**CK** **C**AN SW**I**M. (CK, C, I)
A CAT WI**LL** DR**I**NK SKIM MIL**K**. (LL, I, K)

Pictures Phrases: Procedure, Teacher's Manual page 21: **(Student Workbook page 113-114)**

TACK, MINK, JUNK, SKUNK, JACK IS SICK' MASK, MILK, TRACKS, SKULL.
SAM KICKS A CAN, HIT A TACK, JILL DRINKS MILK. AN ANT SWIMS IN INK.

How many sentences can you make? Procedure, Teacher's Manual page 99: **(Student Workbook page 114) (Use separate lined paper for this exercise)**

CAN, ASK, LICK, MILL, LARK, JACK, SAW, CAT, DUNK, HAVE, VAT, VISTA, JILL, AND, VISIT, HURT, SKULL, **UNDER, WAS, THE, A, UP, AT IT, IS, IN, WAS, WANTS.**

Professor Bloomer's No-Nonsense Reading Program
Lesson 18

Comments: The letter K and the letter C as we are using it have the same sound. Thus the teacher should emphasize the fact that words that end in CK are said the same way as those might be with a double KK

t's time to start reading stories
Read the first story, **Jack and Jill** in Professor Bloomer's No-Nonsense First Phonetic Reader for more practice

---

Special Review:
Sound: Letters G

Words: (TACK, TAG) (SACK, SAG) (JACK, JAG) SLACK, SUCK, TACK, TICK, TUCK, (TUCK, TUG) (DUCK, DUG) (LUCK, LUG) MACK, MICH, MUCK, NICK, RACK, SACK, SICK, (LAG, LACK) (DICK, DIG) CLACK, CLUCK, DICK, DUCK, JACK, KICK, LACK, LUCK.

Shape: Letter   F and H
(KIN, FIN) (KILL, FILL, HILL) (KIT, FIT, HIT) HICK, HACK, HUCK, HUNK, MUSK, MANX, KID, HID, KISS, HISS.

Sentences and phrases: A DUCK CAN SWIM. DAN CAN GIVE MAMA A KISS. SAM KICKS A TIN CAN. JACK WAS SICK. DICK HAD HIS KIT. JACK LACKS SKILL. DICK HAS DIRT IN A SACK. A RAT CAN LICK HIS FUR. JACK HAS A TASK. A CAT AND A LARK HAD A WAR. DICK HAS A KINK IN HIS FIST. IT IS DARK IN A SACK. IF JACK FALLS, HE CAN HURT HIS SKULL. DICK HID A CAT IN A SACK. A MAN CAN SNARE A LARK IN A SACK. MAMA CAN ASK IF JIM SAW JACK.

Professor Bloomer's No-Nonsense Reading Program
Lesson 18

PICTURE PHRASES

TACK

MINK

JUNKS

SKUNK

SICK

MASK

MILK

SKULL

TRACKS

PICTURE PHRASES

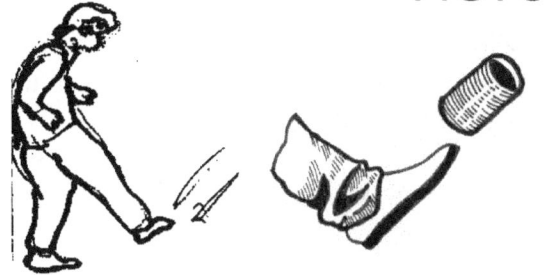

DAN KICKS A CAN

NAN DRINKS MILK

HAMMER A TACK

AN ANT SWIMS IN INK

HOW MANY SENTENCES CAN YOU MAKE?

CAN	ASK	LICK	MILL	A	LARK	JACK	SAW
CAT	DUNK	HAVE	IS	IN	VAT	VISTA	JILL
AND	AT	VISIT	HURT		SKULL		

Lesson 19 The Letter/sound /B/

Purpose: Lesson 19 introduces the Letter/sound /B/ as in BAT and related words. The procedure of this and the following units increases the emphasis on context as related to the meaning of the words.

Timing Note: This lesson should take at least FIVE sessions preferably separated by a whole day. Teachers should judge by the quality of the learner's responses whether to continue on or to rehearse for a longer period. Resting time between learning sessions for consolidation of learning is essential. Remember to start each session with a Review. Time is not important, Quality is.

The Letter/sound /B/: /B/ as in BAT is made by stopping a column of air with the lips and then releasing it. The release is accompanied by a vibration of the vocal chords. An unvoiced /B/ sounds /P/.

Letter formation : B

'B' the capital letter 'B' is formed with three strokes

1. The first stroke is a straight vertical line from the top of the letter to the bottom.

2. The second stroke is an horizontal 'u' shape that begins at the top of the first line and proceeds out to the right returning to connect at the middle of the vertical line.

3. The third stroke is an horizontal 'u' that begins at the connection in the middle of the vertical and proceeds to the right to return and connect at the bottom of the vertical line.

Words: SACK, BAG, BALL, BAM, BAN, BARN, BANK, BLAST, BASK, BAR, BART, BASS, BAT, BIG, BILL, BIN, BIRD, BIT, BLISS, RABBIT, BUCK, BUD, BUG, BULL, BUN, BULB, BUST, BUS, BUT, BUTT, CAB, DUB, NAB, STUB, STAB, TAB, TUB, SLAB, JUMBLE.

Professor Bloomer's No-Nonsense Reading Program
Lesson 19

B_____

_____

PICTURES TO LABEL

BUG

RABBIT

BUN

CUB

BULL

BUS

BAT

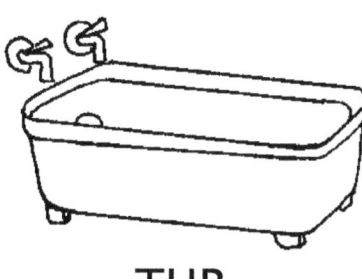
TUB

Professor Bloomer's No-Nonsense Reading Program
Lesson 19

Beginning Review: Procedure, Teachers manual Page 6-7: **(Use separate lined paper for this exercise)**

Review the Letter/sounds /A/ /T/ /S/. /M/ /R/ /G/./F/, /W/, /R/ /N/ /U/, /H/ /J/, /L/. /C/, /I/ /V/. and the words, KID, KILL, KIM, KIN, KINK, KISS, ASK, DARK, JUNK, INK, KIT, LARK, MARK, MASK, RINK, SKULL, SKILL, DRINK, DRANK, LURK, MARK, MILK, MINK, MURK, RANK, RINK, RISK, SANK, SILK, SKAT, SKID, SKIM, SKIN, SKIT, SUNK, TANK, TASK, TURK, TUSK, WINK, WALK, SALT.

The Letter/sound /B/, Procedure: Teacher's Manual page 1; **(Student Workbook page 115)** The letter/sound /B/ as im BOB i

Constructive Synthesis: Procedure: Teacher's Manual page 8; **(Use separate lined paper for this exercise)**

SACK, BAG, BALL, BAM, BAN, BARN, BANK, BLAST, BASK, BAR, BART, BASS, BAT, BIG, BILL, BIN, BIRD, BIT, BLISS, RABBIT, BUCK, BUD, BUG, BULL, BUN, BULB, BUST, BUS, BUT, BUTT, CAB, DUB, NAB, STUB, STAB, TAB, TUB, SLAB, JUMBLE.

Pictures to Label: Procedure Teacher's Manual page 10: **(Student Workbook page 115)**

BUG, RABBIT, BULL, BUN, BAT, CUB, BUS, TUB

Match and Label: Procedure, Teacher's Manual page 21, **(Student Workbook page 116)**

BAT, BUS, DUCK , BUD, BAT, BARK, RABBIT, BIRD, BARN, CRAB, BAT, BALL.

Matching words: Procedure, Teacher's Manual page 16, **(Student Workbook page 117)**

BAT	BUG
BUST	BAT
BUG	SLAB
BULL	BUST
CAB	JIB
RIB	CAB
JIB	RIB
SLAB	BULL

MATCH AND LABEL

BAT
BUS
DUCK
BUD
BARK
RABBIT
BIRD
BARN
CRAB
BUGS
BAT
BALL

CRAB

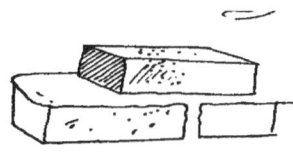
BRICKS

BAT

BUS

BALL

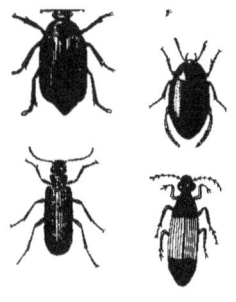
BUGS

RABBIT

DUCKS

BUD

BARN

BARK

BIRD

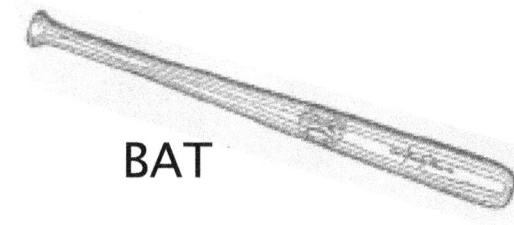
BAT

Professor Bloomer's No-Nonsense Reading Program
Lesson 19

Finding word pairs and Reading Aloud: Procedure, Teacher's Manual page 16, **(Student Workbook page 117)**.

RABBIT	**RABBIT**	BASS	BRAG
BAT	**BACK**	BLAT	**BACK**
BAG	**BUT**	**BUT**	LAB
BULL	RIB	BUS	**BULL**
CAB	**BANK**	STUB	**BANK**
BLAST	BAT	**BLAST**	BRAN
RIB	BUST	**BUG**	**BUG**
BUN	**BUNK**	**BUNK**	BIN
BUG	BIG	**BUG**	BALL
BIRD	**CUB**	BIN	**CUB**

Flash Identification: Procedure, Teacher's Manual page 16: **(Student Workbook page 118)**

Letters to Flash are: **B, D, R, B, G, R, B, K.**

B	**B**IG	DIG	**B**AD	RAG
D	BU**D**	**D**ULL	RAN	BULL
R	DUCK	BA**R**N	BIG	**R**IG
B	**B**UST	DUST	**B**AND	RUST
G	BAD	BUST	**G**UST	BA**G**
R	TA**R**	TAG	TAB	B**R**AN
B	**B**ARD	RA**BB**IT	RAT	STAR
K	DU**CK**	BUN**K**	BID	KID

Sounds in words: Procedure, Teacher's Manual page 16: **(Student Workbook page 118)**

The sequence of Letter/sounds to use in this lesson is as follow
/B/, /C/, /l/, /B/, /G/, /B/, /R/, /D/.

/B/	FILL	MILL	RU**B**	**B**ID	LID
/C/	BRASS	**C**AST	LIST	**C**AB	LIVE
/l/	CAT	SAW	BULB	BRIM	HURT
/B/	SLAM	RU**B**	CRAM	STU**B**	TU**B**
/G/	BU**G**	CART	BRA**G**	CURD	MINT
/B/	RINSE	CRAG	**B**ASS	TRIM	**B**UG
/R/	DUCK	BA**R**D	GUST	B**R**AN	STA**R**
/D/	BA**D**	BARN	**D**UST	BAN**D**	RUST

154

WHAT IS THIS? CAN YOU MAKE IT BETTER?

CAN YOU DRAW IT BETTER DOWN HERE?

Professor Bloomer's No-Nonsense Reading Program
Lesson 19

Dictation: Procedure, Teacher's Manual page 16, **(Student Workbook page 118)** **(Use separate lined paper for this exercise)**

Letter/soundS /A/ /T/ /S/. /M/ /R/ /G/./F/, /W/, /R/ /N/ /U/, /H/ /J/, /L/. /C/, /I/ /V/, /K/, /B/ . and the words, SACK, BAG, BALL, BAM, BAN, BARN, BANK, BLAST, BASK, BAR, BART, BASS, BAT, BIG, BILL, BIN, BIRD, BIT, BLISS, RABBIT, BUCK, BUD, BUG, BULL, BUN, BULB, BUST, BUS, BUT, BUTT, CAB, DUB, NAB, STUB, STAB, TAB, TUB, SLAB, JUMBLE..

Picture completion: Procedure, Teacher's Manual page 46: **(Student Workbook page 119)**

How many words can you make? Procedure, Teacher's Manual page 32: **(Student Workbook page 120)**

The letters are: **B, R, A, C, S, G, T, I, L, N.**

Phrases to Read Aloud and Write: Procedure, Teacher's Manual page 37-38: **(Student Workbook page 120) (Use separate lined paper for this exercise)**

AN ANT BIT A MAN._____
BILL CAN BAT A BALL._____
A SWAN IS A BIG BIRD._____
BART HAS A BUN AND JAM._____
A BULL IS IN A BARN._____
A CRAB CAN'T SWIM ON HIS BACK._____
A RABBIT RAN IN GRASS._____
A BIRD HAS A BILL._____
MAMA CAN RUB A GLASS._____
A RAT WAS IN A BRAN BIN._____
THE HUT WAS IN A JUMBLE._____
A CAT SWAM IN A TUB._____

Professor Bloomer's No-Nonsense Reading Program
Lesson 19

Completing Phrases: Procedure, Teacher's Manual page 38-39: **(Student Workbook page 121)**

BART HAS A **B**UN AND J**A**M. (B, A)
AN ANT B**I**T MAMA. (I)
BILL CAN **B**AT A **B**ALL. (B, B)
DAN CAN D**I**G A **B**IG RUT. (I, B)
MAMA **W**ILL FILL A G**L**ASS. (W, L)
NAN WILL **D**UST A GLASS. (D)
A RABBIT **W**ILL **R**UN IN G**R**ASS. (W, R, R)
A B**U**LL IS IN A BARN. (U)

Pictures to label: Procedure, Teacher's Manual page 21: **(Student Workbook page 121-122)**

BIRD, (CARDINAL) BLOCKS, CABIN, RABBIT, HUMMING BIRD, BRAND, CRAB, CURB, BAT or BUNT, BULL ELK, BURR

How many sentences can you make? Procedure, Teacher's Manual page 99: **(Student Workbook page 122)** **(Use separate lined paper for this exercise)**

BAD, BILL, BUD, BUG, CAN, BUST, DIG, RUN, RABBIT, BIG, BULL, HAS, WAS, NAN, AND, BARN, WENT, IN, SWIM, RAN,. **UNDER, WAS, THE, A, UP, AT IT, IS, IN WANTS.**

Comment: Read the second story **Buster Bug** in Professor Bloomer's No-Nonsense First Phonetic Reader for more practice.

Special Review:
Sound: Letter/sound /D/

Words: (BAM, DAM) (BAD, BUD) (BAG, GAD) (BUST, DUST) (BART, DART) (BAN, DAN) (BUN, DUN) (BUG, DUG) (BUD, DUD) (BIG, DIG) (BID, DID) (BIN, DIN) (BRAG, DRAG) (RIB, RID) (BUNK, DUNK) (LAB, LAD)

Shape: Letters: D R, BAR, BARK BARN, BART, BRAG, BRAN, BRASS, BRAT, BRIM

Words: D's as before. R—(BAT, RAT) (BUM, RUM) BAR (BAG, RAG) (BAN, RAN) (BUST, RUST) (BUG, RUG) RUB (BRAN, RAN) (BRIM, RIM) (BRAG, RUG) (BIG, RIG) (BID, RID) (BACK, RACK) (BARD, BIRD) (BRAD, DRAB) (RUB, RABBIT)

Phrases and sentences. DAN WAS BAD. AN ANT BIT A MAN. A CAB CAN RUN FAST. BILL CAN BAT A BALL. SAM HAS A BAT AND A BALL. DOGS HAVE RIBS. A MARE CAN HAVE BRAN. AN ANT IS A BUG. A SWAN IS A BIG BIRD. A BAT BIT NAN. A CAT WILL GET A BIRD. A BIRD HAS A BILL. DAN IS BIG AND BART IS LITTLE. BILL HAD A BUN AND A JAM TART. A FARM HAS A BIG BULL.

PICTURE PHRASES

BIRD (CARDINAL)

CABIN

RABBIT

HUMMING BIRD

BRAND

CRAB

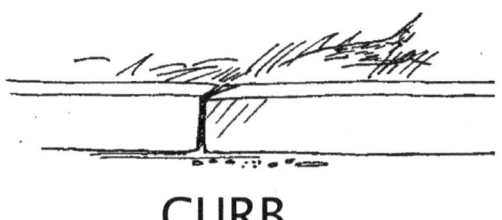
CURB

PICTURE PHRASES

BAT (BUNT)

BULL

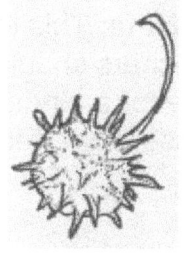
BURR

HOW MANY SENTENCES CAN YOU MAKE?

BAD	BILL	BUD	BUG	CAN	A	BUST	IT	IS
DIG	RUN	RABBIT	BIG	BULL	HAS	WAS	WANTS
NAN	AND	BARN	WENT	IN	SWIM	RAN

Lesson 20 The VOWEL Letter/sound /O/

Purpose: Lesson 20 introduces the fourth vowel Letter/sound /O/ as in HOT and related words. This unit increases the number of available words and sentence construction. The emphasis is upon meaning in a context.

Timing Note: This lesson should take at least FIVE sessions preferably separated by a whole day. Teachers should judge by the quality of the learner's responses whether to continue on or to rehearse for a longer period. Resting time between learning sessions for consolidation of learning is essential. Remember to start each session with a Review. Time is not important, Quality is.

The Letter/sound /O/: /O/as in HOT   /O/ is formed in the lower back of the mouth. The lips are partly opened and the muscles of the mouth are tense. /O/ is what you say when in the doctor's office

Letter formation:
'O' The capital letter 'O' is made with a single curved line

   1. The stroke starts at 2 o'clock and curves to the left in a circular path around to meet at two o'clock to form a circle.

Words: BOG, BOSS, LOG, FOG, FOR, HOT, HORN, JOB, JOT, LOSS, LOST, LOT, LOVE, MOP, MORAL, MORE, MOSS, NOR, NOT, OF, ON, OR, ORAL, OVEN, ROB, RON, ROT, SOB, SON, SOME, SORE, SORT, TOM, TON, TORE, TOSS, TOT.

Procedure: The procedure, because O is a vowel, is somewhat modified from the procedure in Unit 20. The modification recommended is that (1) the introductory period be somewhat longer than in other units and (2) the sound and shape review come between the introductory learning and the sentence material rather than coming when a need arises from them.

Beginning Review: Procedure, Teachers manual Page 6-7: **(Use separate lined paper for this exercise)**

   Letter/sounds /A/ /T/ /S/. /M/ /R/ /G/./F/, /W/, /R/ /N/ /U/, /H/ /J/, /L/. /C/, /I/ /V/, /K/, /B/ . and the words, SACK, BAG, BALL, BAM, BAN, BARN, BANK, BLAST, BASK, BAR, BART, BASS, BAT, BIG, BILL, BIN, BIRD, BIT, BLISS, RABBIT, BUCK, BUD, BUG, BULL, BUN, BULB, BUST, BUS, BUT, BUTT, CAB, DUB, NAB, STUB, STAB, TAB, TUB, SLAB, JUMBLE.

Professor Bloomer's No-Nonsense Reading Program
Lesson 20

Introducing the vowel Letter/sound /O/, Procedure: Teacher's Manual page 1; **(Student Workbook page 123)**

The Letter/sound /O/ as in TOP

Constructive Synthesis: Procedure: Teacher's Manual page 8; **(Use separate lined paper for this exercise)**

BOG, BOSS, LOG, FOG, FOR, HOT, HORN, JOB, JOT, LOSS, LOST, LOT, LOVE, MOP, MORAL, MORE, MOSS, NOR, NOT, OF, ON, OR, ORAL, OVEN, ROB, RON, ROT, SOB, SON, SOME, SORE, SORT, TOM, TON, TORE, TOSS, TOT.

Pictures to Label: Procedure Teacher's Manual page 10: **(Student Workbook page**
COCK, LOCK, DOCK, BOMB, WOLF FROG, DOLL, STORM, WAGON

Match and Label: Procedure, Teacher's Manual page 21, **(Student Workbook page 124)**

DOGS, DOCK, WORM, WORK, HORNS, STORK, WOMAN, HOT DOG, HOT, COLD, GOLF, LOCK.

Matching words: Procedure, Teacher's Manual page 16, **(Student Workbook page 125)**

NOT	WORM
OR	TOSS
HOT	FOR
LOST	SON
BOY	NOT
WORM	BLOT
SON	LOST
TOSS	HOT

Finding word pairs and Reading Aloud: Procedure, Teacher's Manual page 16, **(Student Workbook page 125)**.

FOR	OVEN	**FOR**	TOT
OFF	**DOLL**	**DOLL**	ON
HOT	SON	BORN	SON
TOM	**TOM**	SLOT	WORM
BOSS	**TOSS**	**TOSS**	NOT
BORN	TOT	SLOT	**BORN**
NOT	**MORE**	SON	**MORE**
ROT	OF	**ROT**	OR
OFF	**HOT**	**HOT**	NOT
TOT	**MOM**	BLOT	**MOM**

Professor Bloomer's No-Nonsense Reading Program
Lesson 20

O

PICTURES TO LABEL

COCK

LOCK

DOCK

WOLF

FROG

DOLL

STORM

WAGON

162

MATCH AND LABEL

DOGS
DOCK
WORM
WORK
HORNS
STORK
WOMAN
HOT DOG
HOT
COLD
GOLF
LOCK
TOSS
STORM

Professor Bloomer's No-Nonsense Reading Program
Lesson 20

Flash Identification: Procedure, Teacher's Manual page 46: **(Student Workbook page 126)**

Expose the letters for two (2) seconds Letters to Flash are O, A, C, O, I, D, O, G.

O	FAR	F**O**R	HARM	W**O**RM
A	LOST	FOR	F**A**R	OR**A**L
C	BOG	**C**OT	**C**AT	ON
O	HIT	T**O**M	HAT	H**O**T
I	L**I**ST	LOST	ON	**I**N
D	SOCK	**D**OLL	RAG	**D**IG
O	D**O**G	B**O**ND	DIG	IF
G	DO**G**	COST	HO**G**	DON

Sounds in words: Procedure, Teacher's Manual page 32: **(Student Workbook page 126)**

The sequence to use in this lesson is as follow /O/, /B/, /C/, /R/, /G/, /H/, /L/, /W/.

/O/	B**O**G	LIST	D**O**G	VAST	M**O**P
/B/	COME	**B**OSS	**B**AD	FROG	**B**UT
/C/	**C**AT	DRAM	**C**ROSS	**C**AR	RUB
/R/	SLIT	FOG	SLIM	O**R**	CU**R**T
/G/	FRO**G**	OF	OVEN	**G**OT	**G**ONE
/H/	DOG	WORM	SOCK	LIST	**H**ARM
/L/	BOMD	WARM	**L**OST	DO**LL**	**L**UCK
/W/	DOLL	**W**ON	HOT	SON	BORN

Dictation: Procedure, Teacher's Manual page 16, **(Student Workbook page 126)** **(Use separate lined paper for this exercise)**

Letter/soundS /A/ /T/ /S/. /M/ /R/ /G/./F/, /W/, /R/ /N/ /U/, /H/ /J/, /L/. /C/, /I/ /V/, /K/, /B/, and the WORDS, BOG, BOSS, LOG, FOG, FOR, HOT, HORN, JOB, JOT, LOSS, LOST, LOT, LOVE, MOP, MORAL, MORE, MOSS, NOR, NOT, OF, ON, OR, ORAL, OVEN, ROB, RON, ROT, SOB, SON, SOME, SORE, SORT, TOM, TON, TORE, TOSS, TOT..

Picture completion: Procedure, Teacher's Manual page 46: **(Student Workbook page 127)**

WHAT IS THIS? CAN YOU MAKE IT BETTER?

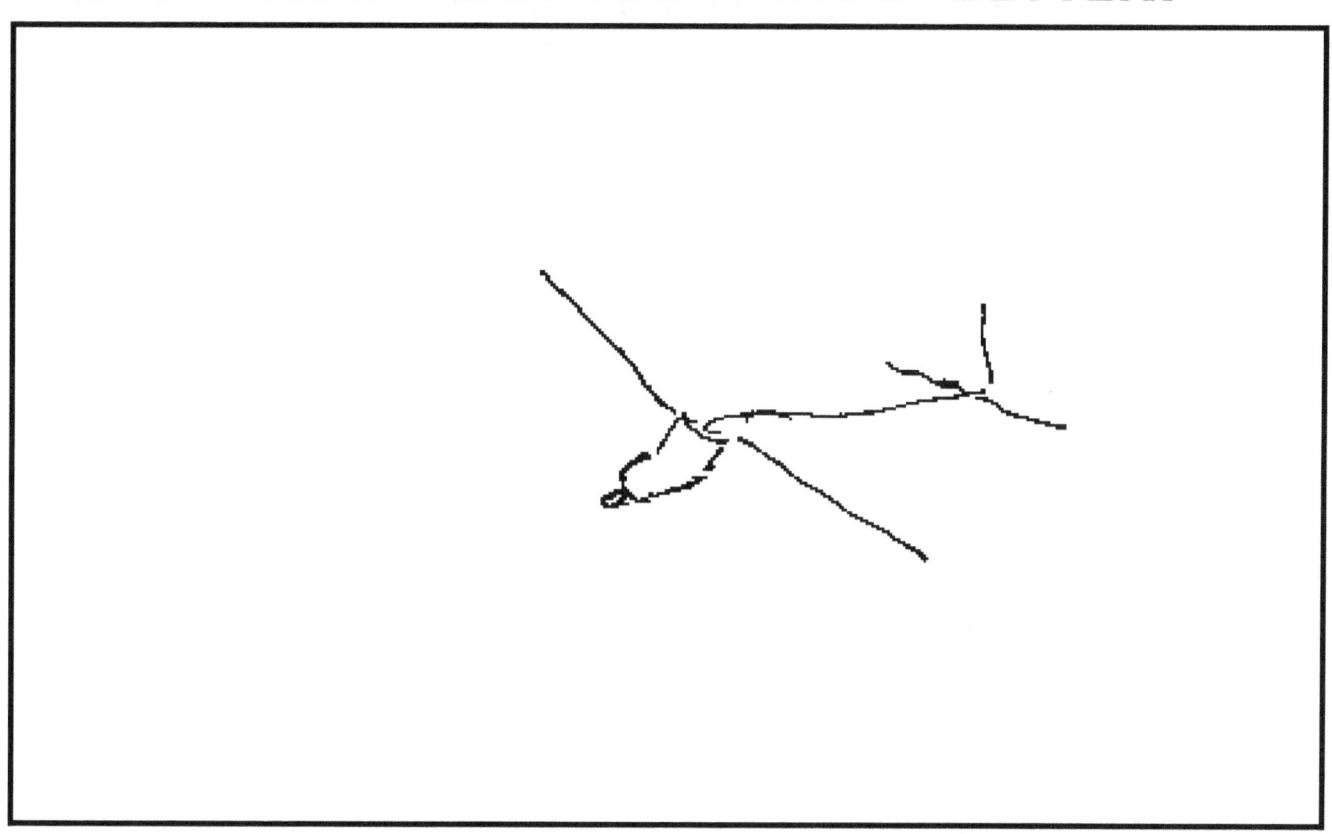

CAN YOU DRAW IT BETTER DOWN HERE?

Professor Bloomer's No-Nonsense Reading Program
Lesson 20

How many words can you make? Procedure, Teacher's Manual page 32: **(Student Workbook page 128)**

The Letter/sounds are: **O, N, I, R, L, V, A, T, U, B.**

Phrases to Read Aloud and Write: Procedure, Teacher's Manual page 37-38: **(Student Workbook page 128) (Use separate lined paper for this exercise)**

A DOG CAN BARK AND WARN A MAN. _____
A FROG SAT ON A ROCK. _____
A BIRD HAD A WORM. _____
NAN LOST HER DOLL. _____
A CAR COSTS A LOT. _____
DON CANNOT COME. _____
A HORSE WILL JOG AND TROT. _____
MOM HAS A HOT BUN FOR TOD. _____
SAM HAS SOME MORE JAM. _____
MOM HAS THE OVEN ON. _____
RON WAS BORN ON A FARM. _____
TOM CAN HAVE A BUN AND A TART. _____
DAN WAS LOST IN A BOG. _____
A HORSE HAS GRASS ON A HILL. _____
A HORSE HAS GONE TO A FARM. _____

Completing Phrases: Procedure, Teacher's Manual page 38-39: **(Student Work book page 129)** . The exercise is designed to increase learner independence and to use context clues to develop meaning.

A FROG SAT ON A ROCK. (O, A, O)
RON WAS BORN ON A FARM. (O)
A CAT WAS WARM. (A)
MAMA HAS A HOT BUN FOR SAM. (O, O)
DAD CALLED A MAN FOR A TON OF SAND. (A, O)
SAM LOST HIS HAT. (O)
A WORM LIVED IN MUD. (O, I)

Professor Bloomer's No-Nonsense Reading Program
Lesson 20

Pictures Phrases; Procedure, Teacher's Manual page 21, **(Student Workbook page 129-130)**
   CANNON, BISON, HOG, HURT ARMOR, DRAGON, WORM, BOBCAT. A CAT HUNTS A RAT. A DOG ON A LOG, AND A CAT IN A LOG. A MAN AND A BULL

How many sentences can you make? Procedure, Teacher's Manual page 99, **(Student Workbook page 130) (Use separate lined paper for this exercise)**
   DOG, FOR, FROG,, BULL, HAVE, IN, BIRD, HAD, A, BRN, WILL, BUN, RUN, SAT, ON, RAT, CAN, NAN, AND, DAN, AFTER, HORSE, WORM, HILL, HOT, **UNDER, OVER, NO,**   WAS, NOT, TO, THE, A, UP, DOWN, AT IT, IS, IN.

Comments: At this point and perhaps before the children and/or the teacher should be able to begin to put the sentences and phrases into order to make short stories

Read the third story **Oliver Drop** in Professor Bloomer's No-Nonsense Phonetic Reader for more practice.

Special review:

Sounds: Letter/sounds /A/ and /I/

Words: (TAM, TAN) (RAT, ROT) (MOSS, MASS) (MORAL) (ON, AN) (FOR, FAR) (RON, RAN) (NOT, NAT) (HAT, HOT) (LAST, LOST) (GLOSS, GLASS) ORAL (ORE, ARE) (ROCK RACK) (LOCK, LUCK) (CAT, COT) (TOT, TAT) (LOSS, LASS) (BOSS, BASS) (SIT, SAT) (MOSS, MISS) (TON, TIM) (FOG, FIG) (NOT, NIT) (HAT, HIT) (LOST, LIST) OF IF (ON, IN) (LOCK, LICK) (TICK, COT, TACK) (SOCK, SICK, SACK)

Shape: Letters C, D, G.

C Words: COCK, CAME, CAST, CAT, CROSS, ROCK, LACK, SOCK, COST, CAST

D Words: DOLL, DON, DONE, DOT, BOND, HAD, LARD, SAD, TAD, TROD, ROD (DOCK, DICK) (ROD, RID) (DON, DIN)

G Words: BAG, FLAG, FOG, GLASS, GONE, GOT, HOT, JOG, LOG, TOG, (FLAG, FLOG) (LOG, LAG) (BOG, BAG)

PICTURE PHRASES

CANNON

BISON

ARMOR

HOG

HURT

WORM

DRAGON

BOBCAT

BLOCKS

A CAT HUNTS A RAT

A DOG ON A LOG

A MAN AND A BULL

HOW MANY SENTENCES CAN YOU MAKE?

DOG	FOR	FROG	AT	BULL	HAVE	IN	BIRD
HAD	A	BARN	WILL	BUN		RUN	SAT
ON	RAT	CAN	NAN	AND		DAN	AFTER
HORSE	WORM		HAS	HILL		HOT	

Professor Bloomer's No-Nonsense Reading Program
Lesson 21

Lesson 21 The Letter/sound /Y/

Purpose: Lesson 21 introduces the Letter/sound /Y/ as in YET and related words. Since /Y/ occurs in our words primarily as an ending, serves the dual purposes of introducing the letter and the ending. The meaning changes that are a function of the ending expand the children's concepts of language relationship. The unit also serves to review the concept of a single sound for double consonants.

Timing Note: This lesson should take at least FOUR sessions preferably separated by a whole day. Teachers should judge by the quality of the learner's responses whether to continue on or to rehearse for a longer period. Resting time between learning sessions for consolidation of learning is essential. Remember to start each session with a Review. Time is not important, Quality is.

Letter/sound /Y as in YET /Y/ is formed with the tongue high in the roof of the mouth. The lips are unrounded and are not tense. The sound is similar to as for /I/.

Letter formation: Y
'Y' The capital 'Y' is made with three straight lines

> 1. The first stroke starts at the top of the letter and angles right, down to the middle of the letter at about 45 degrees.
>
> 2. The second stroke starts at the top of the letter, a letter's width to the right and angles down to meet the first stroke at about 45 degrees.
>
> 3. The third stroke begins in the middle of the letter at the juncture of the first two strokes and proceeds vertically to the bottom of the letter.

Whenever Y is used to make an adjectival form of a noun or verb, it is preceded by two consonants.

Words: BOGGY, BOSSY, BOY, BY, BRASSY, CUDDY, BUGGY, BUNNY, CANDY, CRAGGY, DADDY, DANDY, DANNY, DOGGY, DOLLY, DONNY, DUCKY, DUSTY, FULLY, FUNNY, FURRY, GLASSY, GLOSSY, GUMMY, GUSTY, HANDY, INKY, JAMMY, JIMMY, JOY, KITTY, LADDY, MAMMY, MOMMY, MANY, MISTY, MUDDY, HASTY, NUTTY, RUNNY, SAMMY, RUSTY, SALLY, SANDY, SISSY, SOGGY, SOY, SORRY, STARRY, STUBBY, SUNNY, TACKY, TARRY, TIMMY, TINNY, TOY, VARY

> **Beginning Review:** Procedure, Teachers manual Page 6-7: **(Use separate lined paper for this exercise)**
>
> > Letter/sounds /A/ /T/ /S/. /M/ /R/ /G/./F/, /W/, /R/ /N/ /U/, /H/ /J/, /L/. /C/, /I/ /V/, /K/, /B/, /O/ , and the words, BOG, BOSS, LOG, FOG, FOR, HOT, HORN, JOB, JOT, LOSS, LOST, LOT, LOVE, MOP, MORAL, MORE, MOSS, NOR, NOT, OF, ON, OR, ORAL, OVEN, ROB, RON, ROT, SOB, SON, SOME, SORE, SORT, TOM, TON, TORE, TOSS, TOT.

Professor Bloomer's No-Nonsense Reading Program
Lesson 21

Y _____

_____

PICTURES TO LABEL

BUNNY

YAK

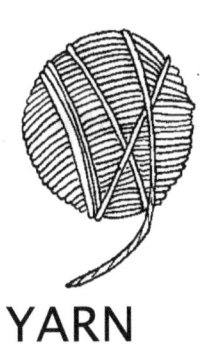
YARN

CRY

KITTY

Professor Bloomer's No-Nonsense Reading Program
Lesson 21

Introducing the Letter/sound /Y/, Procedure: Teacher's Manual page 1; **(Student Workbook page 131)** The Letter/sound /Y/ as oin YET is introduced by showing the learners step by step, how the written letter is formed and having them write it several times while saying the Letter/sound at the same time.

Constructive Synthesis: Procedure: Teacher's Manual page 8; **(Use separate lined paper for this exercise)**

BOGGY, BOSSY, BOY, BY, BRASSY, CUDDY, BUGGY, BUNNY, CANDY, CRAGGY, DADDY, DANDY, DANNY, DOGGY, DOLLY, DONNY, DUCKY, DUSTY, FULLY, FUNNY, FURRY, GLASSY, GLOSSY, GUMMY, GUSTY, HANDY, INKY, JIMMY, JOY, KITTY, LADDY, MAMMY, MOMMY, MANY, MISTY, MUDDY, HASTY, NUTTY,, RUNNY, SAMMY, RUSTY, SALLY, SANDY, SISSY, SOGGY, SOY, SORRY, STARRY, STUBBY, SUNNY, TACKY, TARRY, TIMMY, TINNY, TOY, VARY.

. Given the number of words break this group of words into several short sessions

Pictures to Label: Procedure Teacher's Manual page 10: **(Student Workbook page 131)**

BUNNY YAK YARN CRY KITTY

Match and Label: Procedure, Teacher's Manual page 21, **(Student Workbook page 132)**

CRYING, WAGGY, KITTY, FUNNY, TOY, WINDY, FLY, BUNNY, CANDY,

Matching words: Procedure, Teacher's Manual page 16, **(Student Workbook page 133)**

BY	FURRY
DRY	BUNNY
BUNNY	MANY
FURRY	DRY
MANY	WORRY
WORRY	CANDY
MOMMY	MOMMY
CANDY	BY

MATCH AND LABEL

CRYING
BOY
WAGGY
KITTY
FUNNY
TOY
WINDY
FLY
BUNNY
CANDY
FLYING

TOY

WINDY

KITTY

FLY

CANDY

BUNNY

FLYING

FUNNY

WAGGY

BOY

CRYING

Professor Bloomer's No-Nonsense Reading Program
Lesson 21

Finding word pairs and Reading Aloud: Procedure, Teacher's Manual page 16, **(Student Workbook page 133)**

MISTY	SUNNY	**MISTY**	CANDY
DANDY	**TOY**	DRY	**TOY**
DRY	**DRY**	DOGGY	INKY
DUSTY	NASTY	**BUNNY**	**BUNNY**
CANDY	JIMMY	MUDDY	**CANDY**
DRY	**BY**	**BY**	CANDY
FUNNY	DOGGY	**FUNNY**	SALLY
WORRY	**MISTY**	**MISTY**	DUSTY
JIMMY	DRY	**SOGGY**	**SOGGY**
MOMMY	CANDY	DANDY	**MOMMY**

Flash Identification. Procedure, Teacher's Manual page 46, **(Student Workbook page 134)**

Letters to Flash are: **Y, W, V, Y, N, K, T, Y**

Y	CAN	CAND**Y**	BOG	BO**Y**
W	**W**ORRY	VARY	**W**ARM	BY
V	MISTY	**V**ISTA	**V**ARY	JOY
Y	MAN**Y**	FUN	INK**Y**	STAR
N	DRY	BU**NN**Y	MOMMY	WORRY
K	FRIS**K**Y	LADDY	DANDY	IN**K**Y
T	BOY	MIS**T**Y	S**T**ARRY	DUS**T**Y
Y	DRAG	DR**Y**	TAG	TO**Y**

Sounds in words: Procedure, Teacher's Manual page 32, **(Student Workbook page 134)**

The sequence to use in this lesson is as follow /B/, /O/, /N/, /T/, /R/, /M/, /O/, /Y/.

/B/	DOLLY	**B**OY	**B**RAGGY	**B**ONNY	STU**BB**Y
/O/	DADDY	CANDY	J**O**Y	KITTY	S**O**GGY
/N/	FULLY	MA**N**Y	HA**N**DY	SU**NN**Y	TOY
/T/	GLASSY	FUNNY	S**T**ARRY	SISSY	**T**UBBY
/R/	BONNY	BUDDY	FU**RR**Y	VA**R**Y	**R**USTY
/M/	TIMMY	MUDDY	NASTY	BUNNY	**M**ISTY
/O/	B**O**GGY	DUSTY	GUSTY	GL**O**SSY	W**O**RRY
/Y/	DRAG	FRISK**Y**	DR**Y**	MANY	MIST**Y**

174

Professor Bloomer's No-Nonsende Reading Program
Lesson 21

WHAT IS THIS?   CAN YOU MAKE IT BETTER?

CAN YOU DRAW IT BETTER DOWN HERE?

175

Professor Bloomer's No-Nonsense Reading Program
Lesson 21

Dictation: Procedure, Teacher's Manual page 16,**(Student Workbook page 134)**
(Use separate lined paper for this exercise)

Letter/soundS. /A/ /T/ /S/. /M/ /R/ /G/./F/, /W/, /R/ /N/ /U/, /H/ /J/, /L/. /C/, /I/ /V/, /K/, /B/, /O/, /Y/ and the WORDS, BOGGY, BOSSY, BOY, BY, BRASSY, CUDDY, BUGGY, BUNNY, CANDY, CRAGGY, DADDY, DANDY, DANNY, DOGGY, DOLLY, DONNY, DUCKY, DUSTY, FULLY, FUNNY, FURRY, GLASSY, GLOSSY, GUMMY, GUSTY, HANDY, INKY, JIMMY, JOY, KITTY, LADDY, MAMMY, MOMMY, MANY, MISTY, MUDDY, HASTY, NUTTY, RUNNY, SAMMY, RUSTY, SALLY, SANDY, SISSY, SOGGY, SOY, SORRY, STARRY, STUBBY, SUNNY, TACKY, TARRY, TIMMY, TINNY, TOY, VARY

Picture completion: Procedure, Teacher's Manual page 46, **(Student Workbook page 135)**

How many words can you make? Procedure, Teacher's Manual page 32, **(Student Workbook page 136)**

The letters are **Y, N, U, F, R, S, B, G, D, O.**

Phrases to Read Aloud and Write Procedure, Teacher's Manual page 37-38, **(Student Workbook page 136)** **(Use separate lined paper for this exercise)**

A BOY HAD DIRTY HANDS.
A HUT WAS DUSTY.
A DOGGY IS HUNGRY.
A FRISKY KITTY IS FUNNY.
NAN HAD A DOLLY IN A BUGGY.
DONNY HAD LOTS OF TOYS.
DADDY IS HANDY.
A FURRY BUNNY RAN IN GRASS.
A SANDY LAND WAS DRY AND DUSTY.
SANTA IS JOLLY.
MAMA WILL WORRY IF DAN SWIMS.
MANY DUCKS SWAM IN A RIVER

Professor Bloomer's No-Nonsense Reading Program
Lesson 20

Completing Phrases: Procedure, Teacher's Manual page 38-39, **(Student Workbook page 137)**

SAM HAD A FURRY BUN**NY**. (NY)
A KITTY IS **FU**NNY AND **FU**RRY. (FU, FU)
A FRISKY D**O**G WILL R**U**N. (O, U)
A DO**LL** IS IN A B**U**GGY. (LL, U)
A **B**OY IS A LITTLE **M**AN. (B, M)
DUST IS DR**Y** AND D**I**RTY.. (Y, I)

Pictures to label: Procedure, Teacher's Manual page 16, **(Student Workbook page 137-138)**

BABY (CRIB), CANDY JAR, DRAGON FLY, YAK, DRY DOCK, FLYING, HORSE AND BUGGY

How many sentences can you make? Procedure, Teacher's Manual page 99, **(Student Workbook page 138)** **(Use separate lined paper for this exercise)**

WAS, DOGGY, AND, DIRTY, MUDDY, BUNNY, CAN, FUNNY, KITTY, RAN, SAT, JOLLY, SANTA, FLY, NAN, BUGGY **UNDER, OVER, NO, WAS, NOT, TO, THE, A, UP, DOWN, AT IT, IS, IN.**

Special review: Sound: none
   Shape: Letters W and V

W Words: WORRY, WAGGY, WITTY

V words: VARY

Sentences and phrases: A GUN IS RUSTY. A GUN IS NOT A TOY. MAMA WAS FULL OF WORRY. JIM HAD A DANDY BALL AND BAT. SALLY IS FUNNY. A BOY CAN HAVE MANY TOYS. A RAM IS FURRY BUT A HOG IS NOT FURRY. SALLY WANTS SOME CANDY. DAN'S SOCK WAS MUDDY. IF IT IS SUNNY, IT ISN'T MUDDY. BEN WAS DIRTY AND DUSTY. A LAND WAS SANDY. SALLY WAS A BIG GIRL. SALLY WAS FULL OF JOY. MOMMY IS BOSSY. BEN IS A BRAGGY BOY. SANTA IS A JOLLY MAN.

Professor Bloomer's No-Nonsende Reading Program
Lesson 21

BABY

CANDY

DRAGONFLY

DRY DOCK

YAK

Professor Bloomer's No-Nonsense Reading Program
Lesson 21

FLYING

BUGGY

Comments: The teacher should take advantage of this unit to review the concepts of double letters. Care should be taken to point out the differences in meaning which come as a result of the addition of Y as an ending. For nouns the meaning of adjectives is generally changed by adding the concept likeness to the regular meaning of the word. There are some words which achieve an entirely different meaning when a Y ending is added. Teachers should be careful to draw meaning from the class.

Read the fourth story **The Sticky Kitty** in Professor Bloomer's No-Nonsense First Phonetic Reader for more practice

Professor Bloomer's No-Nonsense Reading Program
Lesson 22

Lesson 22 the Letter/sound /P/

Purpose: Unit XXIII introduces the Letter/sound /P/ and related words. The emphasis of the unit is on comprehension of language units.

Timing Note: This lesson should take at least FIVE sessions preferably separated by a whole day. Teachers should judge by the quality of the learner's responses whether to continue on or to rehearse for a longer period. Resting time between learning sessions for consolidation of learning is essential. Remember to start each session with a Review. Time is not important, Quality is.

Letter/sound, /P/ /P/ as in PAT. /P/ is formed by stopping a column of air with the lips and then releasing it. The vocal chords do not vibrate when /P/ is sounded. A voiced /P/ sounds /B/.

Letter formation: P
P' the capital letter 'P' is made with two lines.

   1. The first stroke is a straight vertical line from the top of the letter to the bottom.

   2. The second stroke is a horizontal 'u' shape that begins at the top of the first line and proceeds out to the right returning to connect at the middle of the vertical line.

Words: ASP, CAP, CRISP, CRISPY, CUB, DIP, GAP, GRASP, HAP, LAP, LIP, LISP, JAP, MAP, LAMP, HAPPY, JAPAN, PACK, JUMP, PUPPY, PICK, PIN, PLUCK, PLUCKY, NAP, PA, PACK, PAL, PAM, PAN, PASS, PAST, PAT, PAW, PIG, PILL, PINK, PIT, PUCK, PUG, PUN, PULL, PUSS, PUT, SAP, SIP, SPIN, SPLIT, SUP, TAP, TIP, TOP, UP, YIP, YIPPY, SPUN.

Procedure: /P/ is introduced, reviews are conducted and sentences and phrases presented as in Lesson 2.

Beginning Review: Procedure, Teachers manual Page 6-7: **(Use separate lined paper for this exercise)**

Letters:/A/ /T/ /S/. /M/ /R/ /G/./F/, /W/, /R/ /N/ /U/, /H/ /J/, /L/. /C/, /I/ /V/, /K/, /B/, /O/, /Y/
and the words, BOGGY, BOSSY, BOY, BY, BRASSY, CUDDY, BUGGY, BUNNY, CANDY, CRAGGY, DADDY, DANDY, DANNY, DOGGY, DOLLY, DONNY, DUCKY, DUSTY, FULLY, FUNNY, FURRY, GLASSY, GLOSSY, GUMMY, GUSTY, HANDY, INKY, JIMMY, JOY, KITTY, LADDY, MAMMY, MOMMY, MANY, MISTY, MUDDY, HASTY, NUTTY, RUNNY, SAMMY, RUSTY, SALLY, SANDY, SISSY, SOGGY, SOY, SORRY, STARRY, STUBBY, SUNNY, TACKY, TARRY, TIMMY, TINNY, TOY, VARY

Introducing the Letter/sound /P/, Procedure: Teacher's Manual page 1; **(Student Workbook page 139)**

   The Letter/sound /P/ as in POP.

P _____

_____

PICTURES TO LABEL

CUP

PANSY

PALM

CAP

PAN

LAMP

PIG

PARK

PICNIC

PLANT

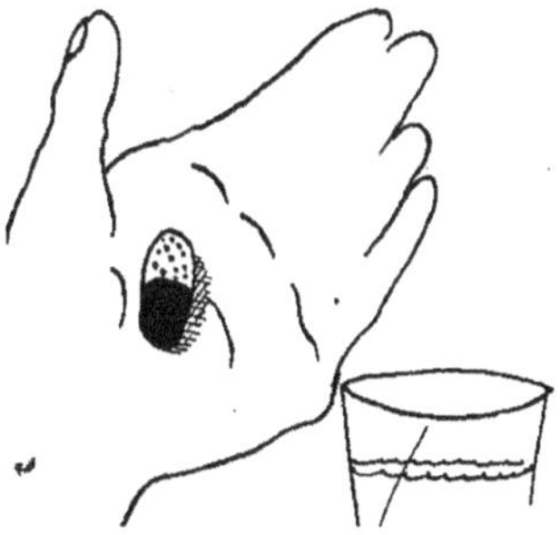

PILL

Professor Bloomer's No-Nonsensde Reading Program
Lesson 22

Constructive Synthesis: Procedure: Teacher's Manual page 8; f **(Use separate lined paper for this exercise)**

ASP, CAP, CRISP, CRISPY, CUB, DIP, GAP, GRASP, HAP, LAP, LIP, LISP, JAP, MAP, LAMP, HAPPY, JAPAN, PACK, JUMP, PUPPY, PICK, PIN, PLUCK, PLUCKY, NAP, PA, PACK, PAL, PAM, PAN, PASS, PAST, PAT, PAW, PIG, PILL, PINK, PIT, PUCK, PUG, PUN, PULL, PUSS, PUT, SAP, SIP, SPIN, SPLIT, SUP, TAP, TIP, TOP, UP, YIP, YIPPY, SPUN.

Pictures to Label: Procedure Teacher's Manual page 10: **(Student Workbook page 139)**

CUP, PANSY, PALM, CAP, PAN, PARK, LAMP, PIG, PLANT, PICNIC, PILL (IN A PALM.)

Match and Labe: Procedure, Teacher's Manual page 21, **(Student Workbook page 140)**
CAP, SPILL, CUP, PIGS, DRIP, PRICK, LIPS, RIP, POP, MOP, CLIP, PICK. JUMP.

Matching words: Procedure, Teacher's Manual page 16, **(Student Workbook page 141)**

CAP	PAL
HAPPY	CUP
PAL	CAP
PULL	PARTY
CUP	HAPPY
PICK	SPOT
PARTY	PICK
SPOT	PULL

Finding word pairs and Reading Aloud: Procedure, Teacher's Manual page 16, **(Student Workbook page 141)**

CAP	**CAP**	PIG	CUP
SPIN	PAW	**PASS**	**PASS**
PANTS	SPILL	**PANTS**	RAT
NAP	**PLUCK**	**PLUCK**	SPIN
MAP	LISP	PIG	**MAP**
PAT	SPOT	**PACK**	**PACK**
PULL	**PATTY**	**PATTY**	PRICK
PILL	**SPUN**	SPILL	**SPUN**
TAP	**TAP**	PICK	MAP
PILL	PRAM	**PILL**	LISP

Professor Bloomer's No-Nonsense Reading Program
Lesson 22

MATCH AND LABEL

CAP
SPILL
CUP
PIGS
DRIP
PRICK
LIPS
RIP
POP
MOP
CLIP
PICK
JUMP

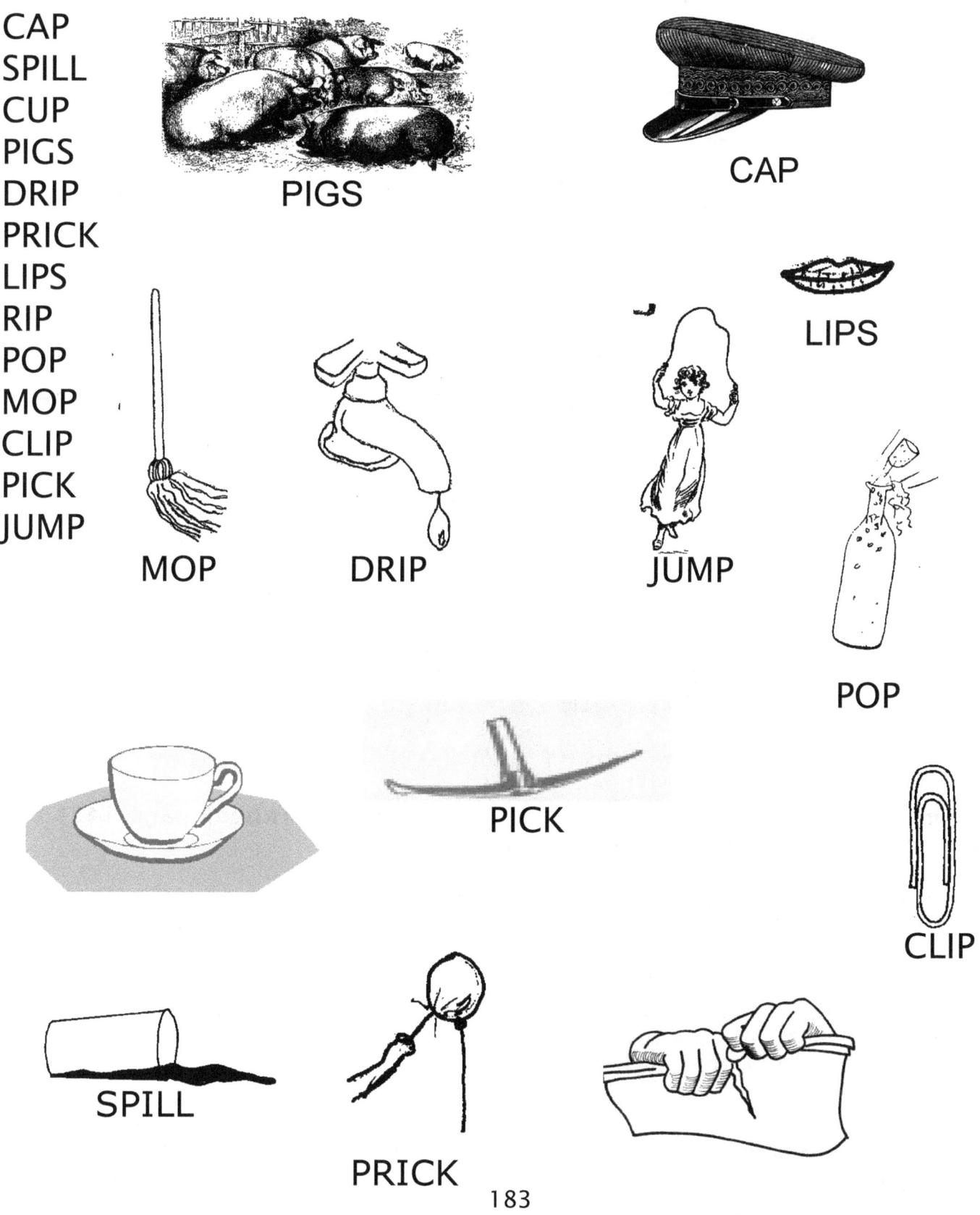

Professor Bloomer's No-Nonsense Reading Program
Lesson 22

Flash Identification: Procedure, Teacher's Manual page 16, **(Student Workbook page 142)**

Letters to Flash are: **P, C, K, O, P. P, L, B,**

P	**P**AST	RAS**P**	ROCK	**P**ACK
C	**C**AP	PIG	**C**AB	BA**C**K
K	SPUD	DIC**K**	SPOT	PIC**K**
O	PORT	TUG	PART	DOCK
P	**P**ILL	TILL	DI**P**	DOCK
P	BIG	**P**ART	RIG	**P**ANT
L	PAD	**L**AD	**L**ID	**L**AP
B	PASS	CUP	**B**ASS	CU**B**

Sounds in words: Procedure, Teacher's Manual page 32, **(Student Workbook page 142)**

The sequence of Letter/sounds to use in this lesson is as follow: /C/, /P/, /L/, /S/, /K/, /P/, /B/, /T/,

/C/	**C**AP	PIG	**C**RISP	PA**C**K	PAT
/P/	RA**P**	RUN	S**P**IT	**P**AL	LA**P**
/L/	**L**ISP	PIT	SIP	PU**LL**	SP**L**IT
/S/	RUT	PA**S**T	PAN	PIG**S**	BACK
/K/	PROD	RIN**K**	POST	PRIM	SIN**K**
/P/	TA**P**	TAB	**P**AT	MAD	**P**OT
/B/	PASS	CUP	**B**ASS	CU**B**	PART
/T/	SPOR**T**	TUG	PA**T**	SPO**T**	PACK

Dictation: Procedure, Teacher's Manual page 16, **(Student Workbook page 142)** **(Use separate lined paper for this exercise)**

Letter/sound**S**, /A/, /T/, /S/, /M/, /R/, /G/,/F/, /W/, /R/, /N/, /U/, /H/, /J/, /L/, /C/, /I/, /V/, /K/, /B/, /O/, /Y/, /P/.
and the WORDS, ASP, CAP, CRISP, CRISPY, CUB, DIP, GAP, GRASP, LAP, LIP, LISP, JAP, MAP, LAMP, HAPPY, JAPAN, PACK, JUMP, PUPPY, PICK, PIN, PLUCK, PLUCKY, NAP, PA, PACK, PAL, PAM, PAN, PASS, PAST, PAT, PAW, PIG, PILL, PINK, PIT, PUCK, PUG, PUN, PULL, PUSS, PUT, SAP, SIP, SPIN, SPLIT, SUP, TAP, TIP, TOP, UP, YIP, YIPPY, SPUN.

Picture completion: Procedure, Teacher's Manual page 46, **(Student Workbook page 143)**

WHAT IS THIS? CAN YOU MAKE IT BETTER?

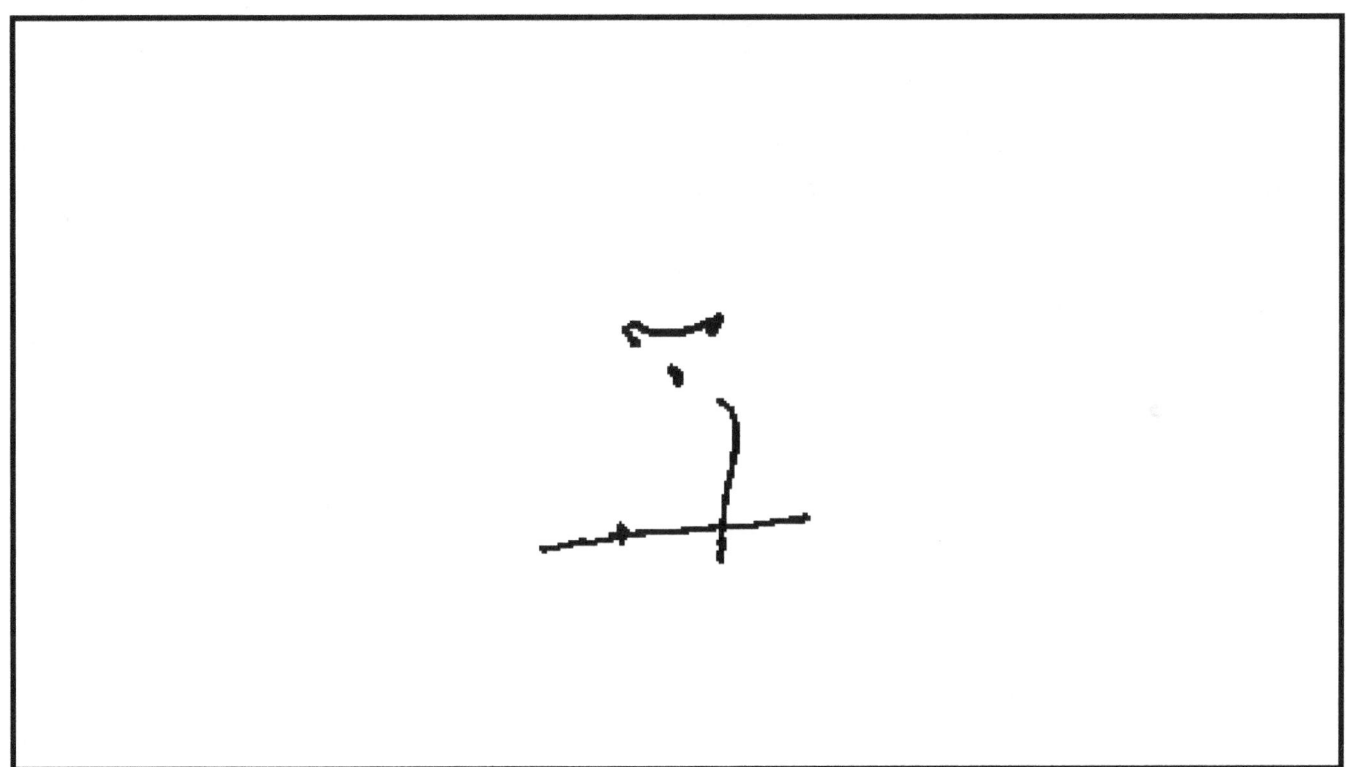

CAN YOU DRAW IT BETTER DOWN HERE?

Professor Bloomer's No-Nonsense Reading Program
Lesson 22

How many words can you make? Procedure, Teacher's Manual page 16, **(Student Workbook page 144)**

The letters are: **P, A, R, T, I, N, K, V, Y, U.**

Phrases to Read and Write: Procedure, Teacher's Manual page 37-38, **(Student Workbook page 144) (Use separate lined paper for this exercise)**

A BRASS BAND WAS IN A PARK_____
A BUNNY JUMPED IN A POND._____
A MAN HAD BLACK PANTS AND CAP._____
A KITTY IS PURRY._____
SALLY DRANK FROM A CUP._____
PAT LIT A LAMP._____
A FARM HAD A BIG CORN CROP._____
MAMA PUT A PIN IN A RIP IN SAM'S PANTS._____
DAN AND PAT WILL SWAP CAPS._____
THE POND IS PAST THE BARN._____
DAN HAD HIS PACK ON A WALK._____
TIPPY IS A HAPPY PUPPY._____

Completing Phrases: Procedure, Teacher's Manual page 38-39, **(Student Workbook page 145)**

The exercise is designed to increase learner independence and to use context clues to develop meaning.

SPORTS ARE **F**UN. (F)
A **FU**LL DOG IS **HA**PPY. (U, HA)
A **C**AT HAD A **N**AP. (C, N)
A **P**IG IS H**U**NGRY FOR **C**ORN. (P, U, C)
A **D**OG HURT HIS **P**AW. (D, P)
NAN P**U**T A LI**D** ON A JAR. (U, D)
SAM **H**AD A **B**IG BALL. (H, B)

Pictures Phrases: Procedure, Teacher's Manual page 16, **(Student Workbook page 145-46)**

POPPY, POTATO, PUMPKIN, PLUM, PIE, PEPPER, HARP, PEPPERS BUG (PRAYING MANTIS) PING PONG, OCTOPUS, PARROT TURNIP, HIPPO (HIPPOPOTAMUS)

Professor Bloomer's No-Nonsensading Program
Lesson 22

How many sentences can you make? Procedure, Teacher's Manual page 99, **(Student Workbook page 146) (Use separate lined paper for this exercise)**

DAN, PARTY, AND, PAT, , PIG, HAD, KITTY, PURR, DIG, CAN, PARK, JUMPED, POND, SPOT, PACK, POTATO, PARROT, **UNDER, OVER, NO, WAS, NOT, TO, THE,** A, UP, DOWN, AT IT, IS, IN.

Comment: Read the fifth story **Copper Penny** in Professor Bloomer's No-Nonsense Phonetic Reader for more practice .

Special Review:
Sound Letter/soundS: /B/, /D/, /T/.

Words: (BUT, PUT) (BASS, PASS) (PAM, BAM) (PAR, BAR) (MAD, BAD) (PART, DART) (PAN, BAN) (PUN, BUN) (PIT, BIT) (PRIM, BRIM) (PUS, BUS) (PACK, BACK) (BUCK, DUCK) (PAT, BAT) (RAB, TAB) (GAP, GAB) (JAP, JAB) (NAP, NAB) (PUG, BUG) (PURR, BURR) (PALL, BALL) (PULL, BULL) (PIG, BIG) (PILL, BILL) (RIP, RIB) (PIN, BIN) (CAP, CAB) (PUMP, BUNK) (CUP, CUD) (PAM, DAM) (PAD, DAD) (PAM, DAN) (PART, DART) (PUN, DUN) (BAD, PAD) (PIG, DIG) (PUCK, DUCK) (MAP, MAD) (PIN, DIN) (TAB, TAD) (SAP, SAD) (LIP, LID) (WARP, WARD) (RIP, RID) (DIP, DID) (CAP, CAD) (CUP, CUD) (PUNK, DUNK) (PUT, PAM, TAM) (PAR, TAR) (PRIM, TRIM) (SPIT, SPLIT) PART (PAD, TAD) (MAN, TAN) (PUG, TUG) (PUB, TUB) (TAP, PAT) (PUCK, TUCK) (PACK, TACK) (MAT, MAP) (HAP, PAT) (SIP, SIT) (SAP, SAT) (RAP, RAT) (GAP, GAT) (NAP, NAT) (CUP, CUT) (TIM, PIT)

Shape review: Letters: B D R
  Words:
  B.   BOP, PUB PAD, POD, DIP, SPUD

  T   PANT, POST, PAST, PAT, PATTY, POT, PUT, SPOT, TAP, TOP, TIP, TIPPY

  R   CARP, CRISP, CRISPY, CROP, GRASP, GRASPY, PAR, PRAM, PRIM, PRICK, PROM, PAR, PURRY, RAP, RASP, RIP, SPAR, SPUR, WARP, PARK, PRINT. (PAM, RAM) (PAR, RAP) (PAW, RAW) (PART, PAN, RAN) (PUN, RUN) PRESS, PARTLY, PRIM, (PUG, RUG) PURR, PROD, (PIG, RIG) GRASP, WARP (JAP, JAR) RIP (CAP, CAR) (CUP, CUR) (PINK, RINK) CRISP, PORT, PRAM, PRICK, PARTY, PROM, SPAR, RASP, TARP, STRAP, SPORT

  More than 1: PARTY, PART, PORT, PROD, SPORT, TARP

Sentences and phrases: "PASS THE DUCK," ASKED JACK. SLIM PANTS CAN'T FIT A FAT MAN. A CAT CAN PURR. SAM PATS HIS DOG. A BULL CAN PULL A ROCK. A WASP CAN HURT. PAT MUST HAVE A NAP. SAM SPLIT HIS LIP. DAN HAD PART OF A BUN. MAMA HAD A PAN OF TARTS. JACK AND JILL RAN UP A HILL. BOB AND DAN SPIN TOPS. BEN PUT A BIRD IN A JAR. DAN HAS A PINK CUP. SAM CAN PACK HIS BAG. MAMA WILL GIVE A PARTY. A TART IS CRISP. A LID IS PART OF A PAN. DAN HAS A PASS. NAN SAT ON DAD'S LAP

PICTURE PHRASES

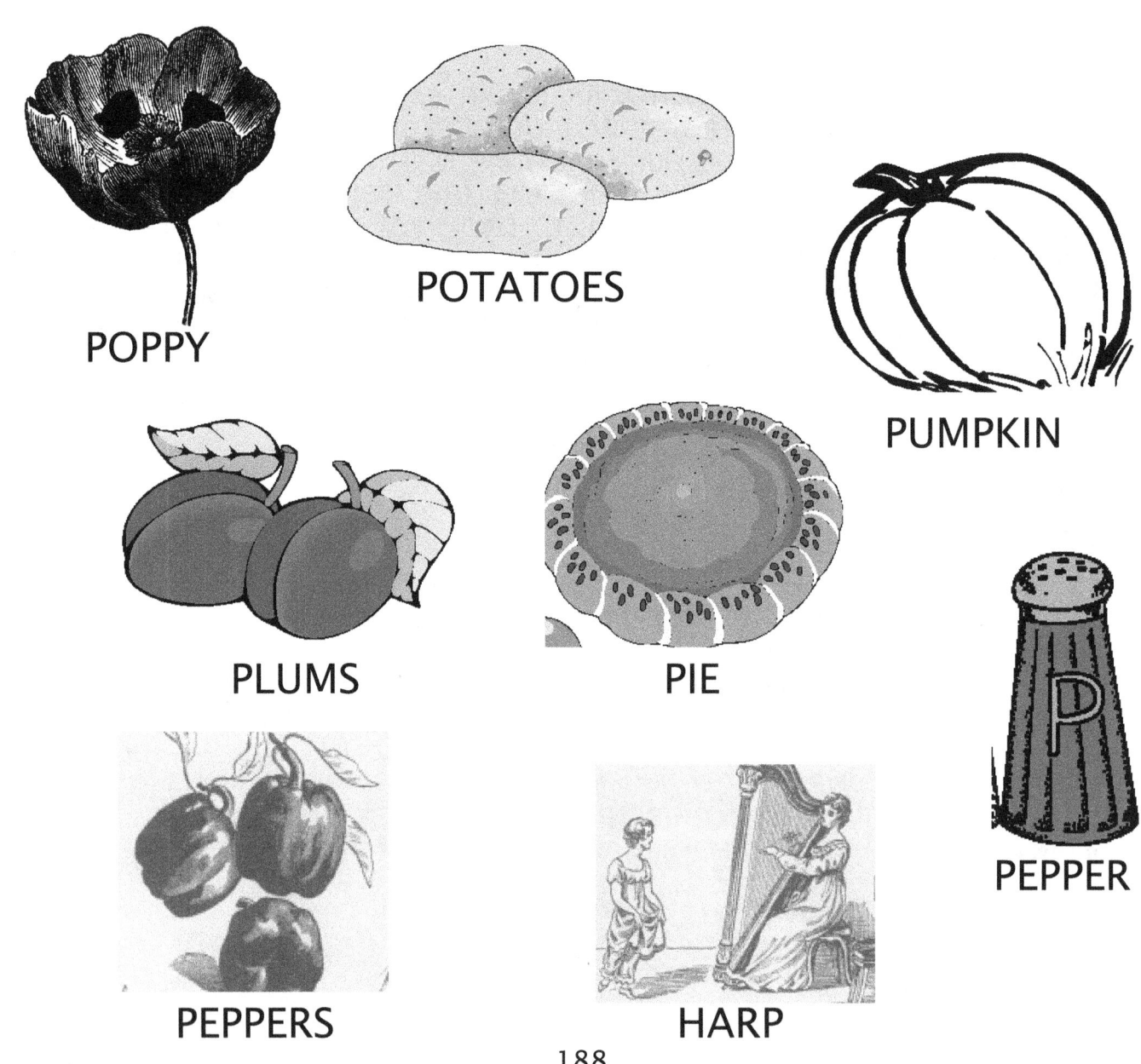

POPPY   POTATOES   PUMPKIN

PLUMS   PIE   PEPPER

PEPPERS   HARP

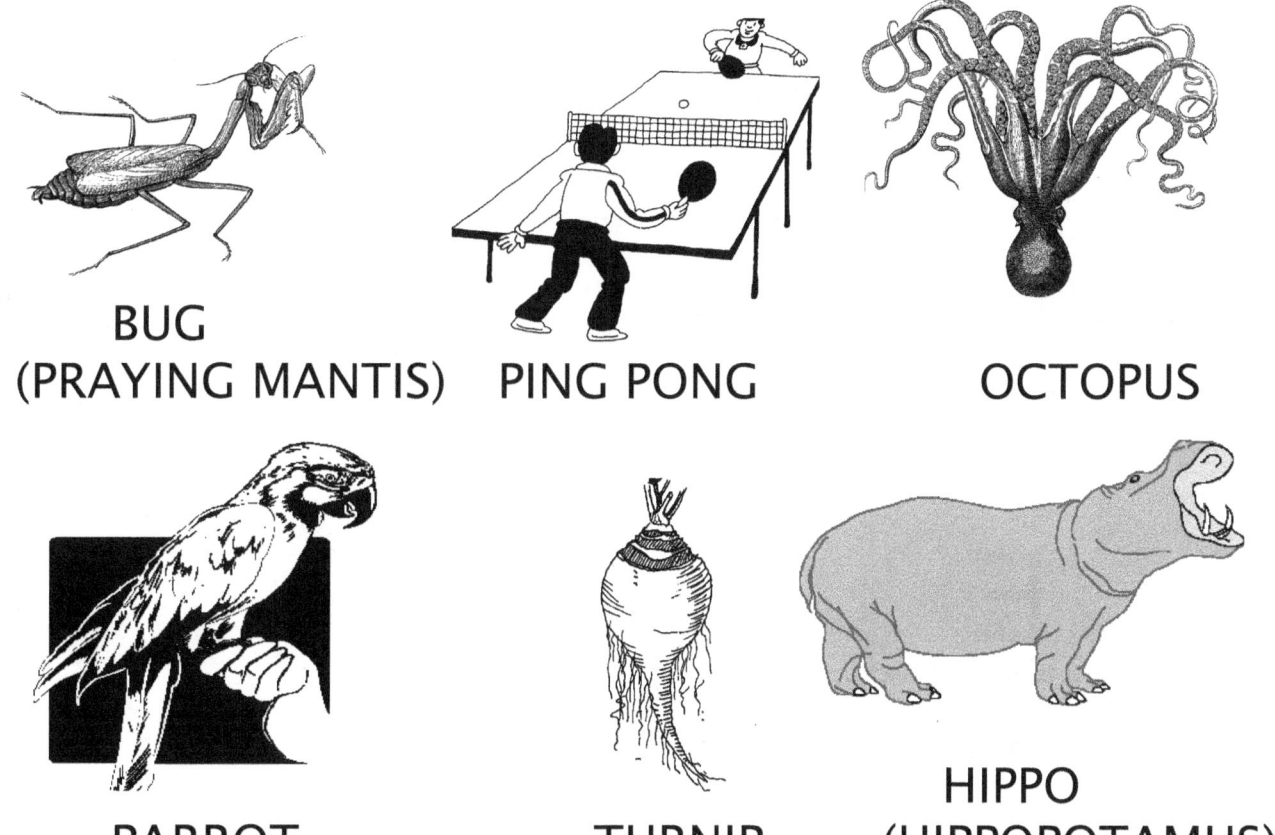

Professor Bloomer's No-Nonsense Reading Program
Lesson 23

Lesson 23 the VOWEL Letter/sound /E/

Purpose: Lesson 24 introduces the vowel Letter/sound /E/ as in MET and related words. The emphasis of this unit is primarily on learning the sound of this letter and learning to tell it from the others. /E/ is the most difficult of the vowel sounds to learn. The number of words which are available by the addition of this particular vowel is almost the complete requirement for the year. The children should be able to put the words they have learned to constructive use in making stories.

Timing Note: This lesson should take at least SIX sessions preferably separated by a whole day. Teachers should judge by the quality of the learner's responses whether to continue on or to rehearse for a longer period. Resting time between learning sessions for consolidation of learning is essential. Remember to start each session with a Review. Time is not important, Quality is.

Letter/sound. /E/. /E/ as in MET is formed in the middle of the front of the mouth with the lips unrounded and not tense. The mouth is slightly more closed than for /A/ and slightly less closed than for /I/.

Letter Formation:
'E' The capital letter 'E' is composed of four straight lines

    1. The first stroke is a vertical line from the top to the bottom of the letter.

    2. The second stroke is half the length of the first. It starts at the top of the vertical line and proceeds perpendicular to the right.

    3. The third stroke is half the length of the first. It starts at the middle of the vertical line and proceeds perpendicular to the right.

    4. The fourth stroke is half the length of the first. It starts at the bottom of the vertical line and proceeds perpendicular to the right.

Words; AFTER, BED, BEG, BELL, BEN, BEST, BET, DELL, DEN, DRESS, EGG, ELF, ELM, ELSE, END, FED, EVER, FELL, GET, GLEN, HELP, HEW, HEN, HER, JELL, LED, JELLY, LEG, LEND, LENT, JEST, LESS, JESUS, LEST, JET, LET, LINEN, KEG, MEN, MESS, MET, METAL, NECK, NEST, NET, NEVER, PEG, PEN, RED, PEST, RENT, PET, REST, SELF, SEND, SENT, SERUM, SEVEN, SET, SELL, STEM, TELL, TEN, TENSE, TEST, VERSE, SISTER, VEST, VET, WATER, WED, WENT, WERE, VERY, WELL, WEST, WET.

Professor Bloomer's No-Nonsense Reading Program
Lesson 23

E _____

_____

PICTURES TO LABEL

PEN

BUTTER

BELL

APPLE

ELF

BASKET

BERRY

DINNER

GARDEN

NEST

SLED

TURTLE

Professor Bloomer's No-Nonsense Reading Program
Lesson 23

Beginning Review: Procedure, Teachers manual Page 6-7: **(Use separate lined paper for this exercise)**

/A/ /T/ /S/. /M/ /R/ /G/./F/, /W/, /R/ /N/ /U/, /H/ /J/, /L/. /C/, /I/ /V/, /K/, /B/, /O/, /Y/, /P/ and the words, ASP, CAP, CRISP, CRISPY, CUB, DIP, GAP, GRASP, HAP, LAP, LIP, LISP, MAP, LAMP, HAPPY, JAPAN, PACK, JUMP, PUPPY, PICK, PIN, PLUCK, PLUCKY, NAP, PA, PACK, PAL, PAM, PAN, PASS, PAST, PAT, PAW, PIG, PILL, PINK, PIT, PUCK, PUG, PUN, PULL, PUSS, PUT, SAP, SIP, SPIN, SPLIT, SUP, TAP, TIP, TOP, UP, YIP, YIPPY, SPUN.

Introducing the vowel Letter/sound /E/, Procedure: Teacher's Manual page 1; **(Student Workbook page 147)**, The vowel Letter/sound /E/ is as in EVER is introduced by showing the learners step by step, how the written letter is formed and having them write it several times while saying the Letter/sound at the same time.

Constructive Synthesis: Procedure: Teacher's Manual page 8; **(Use separate lined paper for this exercise)**

AFTER, BED, BEG, BELL, BEN, BEST, BET, DELL, DEN, DRESS, EGG, ELF, ELM, ELSE, END, FED, EVER, FELL, GET, GLEN, HELP, HEW, HEN, HER, JELL, LED, JELLY, LEG, LEND, LENT, JEST, LESS, JESUS, LEST, JET, LET, LINEN, KEG, MEN, MESS, MET, METAL, NECK, NEST, NET, NEVER, PEG, PEN, RED, PEST, RENT, PET, REST, SELF, SEND, SENT, SERUM, SEVEN, SET, SELL, STEM, TELL, TEN, TENSE, TEST, VERSE, SISTER, VEST, VET, WATER, WED, WENT, WERE, VERY, WELL, WEST, WET.

Pictures to Label: Procedure Teacher's Manual page 10: **(Student Workbook page 147)**

PEN, BUTTER, BELL, APPLE, ELF, BASKET, BERRY, DINNER, GARDEN, NEST, SLED, TURTLE

Match and Label: Procedure, Teacher's Manual page 21, **(Student Workbook page 148)**

BED, HEN, ELK. TURKEY, BUCKET, DONKEY, DRESS, BELL, EGG, KEG, MONKEY, ELF

Professor Bloomer's No-Nonsense Reading Program
Lesson 23

MATCH AND LABEL

BED
HEN
ELK
TURKEY
BARREL
DONKEY
DRESS
BELL
EGGS
KEG
MONKEY
ELF

Professor Bloomer's No-Nonsense Reading Program
Lesson 23

Matching words: Procedure, Teacher's Manual page 16, **(Student Workbook page 149)**

RED	DECK
DRESS	VERY
DECK	NEVER
NEVER	WERE
VERY	HER
EVERY	DRESS
HER	EVERY
WERE	RED

Finding word pairs and Reading Aloud: Procedure, Teacher's Manual page 16, **(Student Workbook page 149)**

VERSE	EVER	HEN	**VERSE**
BLESS	**SEVEN**	**SEVEN**	RED
END	**END**	MESS	DECK
HER	WERE	**HER**	PECK
RED	BESS	**DRESS**	**DRESS**
WENT	WERE	WANT	**WENT**
SEND	SENT	EVERY	**SEND**
DECK	**NECK**	**NECK**	NED
LINEN	**DEN**	**DEN**	SEVEN
BED	**BED**	BEG	VERY

Flash Identification: Procedure, Teacher's Manual page 46, **(Student Workbook page 150)**

Letters to Flash are: **E, A, E, F, O, I, P, E, B, V.**

E	S**E**ND	SAND	AFT**E**R	AND
A	B**A**ND	W**A**TER	D**A**N	DEN
E	B**E**D	BAD	LID	L**E**D
F	HER	EL**F**	**F**ED	WET
O	LET	DECK	L**O**T	BECK**O**N
I	B**I**G	LINEN	LET	BEG
P	**P**EST	BET	BEST	**P**EG
E	F**E**LL	WANT	MOSS	FILL
B	PIG	**B**EN	PEN	**B**ELL
V	RENT	LESS	**V**EST	ELM

Professor Bloomer's No-Nonsense Reading Program
Lesson 23

Sounds in words: Procedure, Teacher's Manual page 32, **(Student Workbook page 150)**

The sequence of Letter/sounds in this lesson is as follow   /F/, /S/, /P/, /L/, /R/, /F/, /P/, /L/, /E/.

/F/	A**F**TER	HE**R**	EL**F**	**F**ED	WET
/S/	TEN	**S**ENT	**S**EVEN	BED	**S**ELF
/P/	BEST	SERUM	HEL**P**	**P**EST	**P**EG
/L/	BE**LL**	HEN	JE**LL**Y	**L**EST	STEM
/R/	GET	**R**ENT	LESS	VEST	ELM
/F/	WENT	**F**ELL	**F**ILL	WET	MEN
/P/	WANT	MOSS	**P**EST	**P**IG	BEN
/L/	**L**INEN	**L**ET	BIG	PEST	BET
/E/	BAD	LID	L**E**D	H**E**R	**E**LF

Dictation: Procedure, Teacher's Manual page 16, **(Student Workbook page 150)** **(Use separate lined paper for this exercise)**

Letter/soundS   /A/ /T/ /S/. /M/ /R/ /G/./F/, /W/, /R/ /N/ /U/, /H/ /J/, /L/. /C/, /I/ /V/, /K/, /B/, /O/, /Y/, /P/, /E/
and the WORDS, AFTER, BED, BEG, BELL, BEN, BEST, BET, DELL, DEN, DRESS, EGG, ELF, ELM, ELSE, END, FED, EVER, FELL, GET, GLEN, HELP, HEW, HEN, HER, JELL, LED, JELLY, LEG, LEND, LENT, JEST, LESS, JESUS, LEST, JET, LET, LINEN, KEG, MEN, MESS, MET, METAL, NECK, NEST, NET, NEVER, PEG, PEN, RED, PEST, RENT, PET, REST, SELF, SEND, SENT, SERUM, SEVEN, SET, SELL, STEM, TELL, TEN, TENSE, TEST, VERSE, SISTER, VEST, VET, WATER, WED, WENT, WERE, VERY, WELL, WEST, WET.

Picture completion: Procedure, Teacher's Manual page 46, **(Student Workbook page 151)**

How many words can you make? Procedure, Teacher's Manual page 32, **(Student Workbook page 152)**

The letters are **E, L, N, M, S, T, D, B, O, P**

WHAT IS THIS?   CAN YOU MAKE IT BETTER?

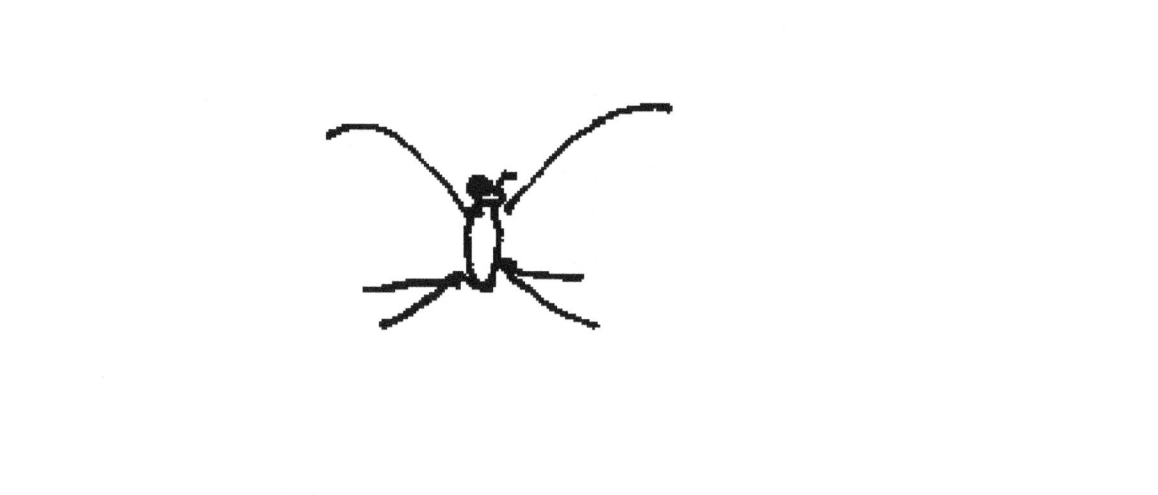

CAN YOU DRAW IT BETTER DOWN HERE?

Professor Bloomer's No-Nonsense Reading Program
Lesson 23

Phrases to Read Aloud and Write: Procedure, Teacher's Manual page 37-38, **(Student Workbook page 152) (Use separate lined paper for this exercise)**

AN ANT IS A PEST. _____
A BRASS ROD WILL BEND. _____
MEG HAS A GLASS OF WATER. _____
A HORSE HAS GRASS FOR DINNER. _____
A HORSE HAD A STRAW BED. _____
A DOG WILL BEG HIS DINNER. _____
SAM HAD A TENT BY A RIVER _____
DAN SLEPT ON A COT . _____
BOYS AND GIRLS ARE MERRY AT A PARTY. _____
NAN HAD HER BEST DRESS _____
DAN FELL IN A RIVER AND WAS VERY WET _____
HE FED A PET PIG _____
A HEN HAD AN EGG _____
A HEN PUT AN EGG IN A NEST _____
NAN WANTS EGGS AND DAN WILL GET HER SOME. _____
 MAMA WILL NEVER GIVE TOM A BAD EGG. _____

Completing Phrases: Procedure, Teacher's Manual page 38-39, **(Student Workbook page 153)**

A DOG WILL G**E**T V**E**RY HUNGRY. (E, E)
A P**I**G IS KEPT IN A P**E**N. (I, E)
SAM HURT H**I**S L**E**G. (I, E)
NAN HAS A **R**ED DRESS. (R)
A W**E**T BUN IS SOG**GY**. (E, GY)
DAN WAS B**A**D AND WENT TO B**E**D. (A, E)
SAM H**A**S A BALL AND A B**A**T. (A, A)
BILL W**A**NTS TO VIS**I**T SALLY. (A, I)

Pictures Phrases: Procedure, Teacher's Manual page 16, **(Student Workbook page 153-154)**

VEST, GAVEL, LOBSTER, FUNNEL, BERRIES, OTTER, CAMEL, HELMET, GRASSHOPPER, CARPET, DOG, PUPPET, BUTTERFLY, JESTER, FERRT

How many sentences can you make? Procedure, Teacher's Manual page 99, **(Student Workbook page 154) (Use separate lined paper for this exercise)**

WEST, HAD, ELF, WAS, AND, NAN, SAT, DRESS, SENT, PAT, A, IS, PARTY, HER, AN, STUMP, NEST, HEN, WENT, PECK, WOLF, RIVER. **UNDER, OVER, NO, WAS, NOT, TO, THE, IN, UP, DOWN, AT, IT.**

Professor Bloomer's No-Nonsense Reading Program
Lesson 23

Special Review: Unit XXIV

Letters: Letter/sounds to Review: /A/, /I/, /O/, /E/.

Words: SET, SAT, SIT; MET, MAT,,MIT; GET, GOT; WERE, WORE; TEN, TAN, TIN, TON; DEN, DAN, DIN, DON; MEN, MAN; NET, NAT, NIT, NOT; HEM, HAM, HIM; LEG, LAG, LOG; LEST, LAST, LIST, LOST; FELL, FALL, FILL; DELL, DILL, DOLL; HELL, HALL, HILL; WET, WIT; VET VAT; VEST, VAST: MESS, MASS, MISS, MOSS; WELL, WALL, WILL; TELL, TALL, TILL; LET, LIT, LOT; NECK, NICK; BESS, BASS, BOSS; BEG, BAG, BIG, BOG; BELL. BALL, BILL; PET, PAT, PIT, POT; PEST, PAST, POST; JET, JOT; FED, FAD, LED, LAD, LID; LESS, LASS, LOSS; RED, RID, ROD; PER, PAR.

Letter: Review for shape: E, F, L, T.

Words: FELL, SELL, WENT, SELF, FED, LEG, BET, FED, BET, PERT, LEND, TEN, LET, TELL, JELL, PET, ELM, JET, ELSE, NEST, LINEN, METAL, LESS, MERIT, LENT, VEST, LED, MET, SET, SENT.

Phrases and Sentences: NAN MUST PRESS HER DRESS. DAN MET BESS AT A BALL. NAN PUT A HEM IN HER DRESS. DAN WILL SELL JELLY TARTS. MAMA HAS A RED LINEN DRESS. A VET CAN HELP A SICK DOG. A HEN CAN SIT ON A NEST OF EGGS. DAD HAS A HERD ON HIS FARM. A RAFT SANK IN MUDDY WATER. AN ANT FELL IN SOME JAM. AN ELF IS FULL OF FUN. PEG WAS PUT IN BED AFTER DINNER. BERT HAS A RED VEST. A BIRD HAS A NEST OF EGGS. DAN LENT HIS BEST HAT. TOM CAST HIS NET IN SOME WATER. BESS AND MEG WERE IN BED AT SEVEN. HE FED A PET PIG. A HEN HAD AN EGG. TOM WILL NOT TOSS AN EGG TO DAN. A WET CRUST IS SOGGY. NAN HAD HER BEST DRESS. A HEN PUT AN EGG INTO A NEST. SAM HAD A TENT BY A RIVER.

Comments: Of all the vowel sounds the letter E is more easily confused with each of the other vowels than any other vowel. Thus, it i may require extra effort.

PICTURE PHRASES

VEST

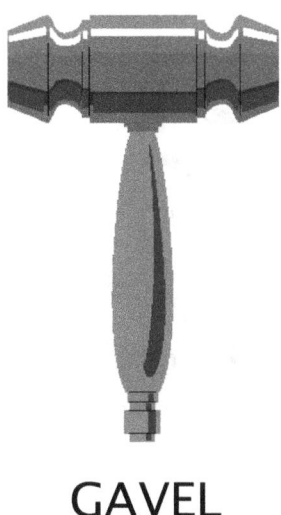
GAVEL

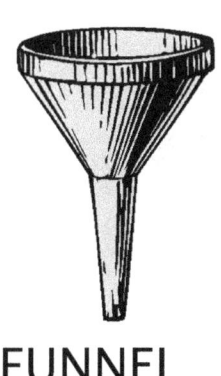
FUNNEL

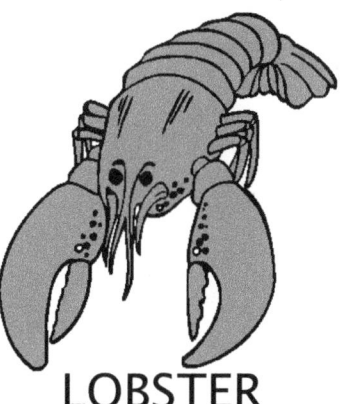
LOBSTER

BERRIES

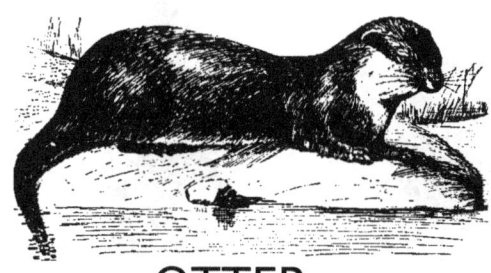
OTTER

CAMEL

HELMET

GRASSHOPPER

Professor Bloomer's No-Nonsense Reading Program
Lesson 23

CARPET

BEG (DOG)

PUPPET

BUTTERFLY

JESTER

FERRET

Comment: Read the story **Copper Penny** in Professor Bloomer's No-Nonsense Phonetic Reader for more practice

Professor Bloomer's No-Nonsense Reading Program
Lesson 24

Lesson 24 The Letter/sound /Z/

Purpose: Unit XXV introduces the letter Z as in ZOO and related words. Since the amount of work required and the number of new words is small, the major purpose of the unit is to consolidate the gains of the previous material.

Timing Note: This lesson should take at least THREE sessions preferably separated by a whole day. Teachers should judge by the quality of the learner's responses whether to continue on or to rehearse for a longer period. Resting time between learning sessions for consolidation of learning is essential. Remember to start each session with a Review. Time is not important, Quality is.

Letter/sound /Z/ as in ZOO. /Z/ is formed by placing the tip of the tongue close to the roof of the mouth. Just behind the upper front teeth a column of air is forced between the tongue and the teeth. This is accompanied by a vibration of the vocal chords. Unvoiced /Z/ sounds /S/.

Letter Formation: Z

'Z' the capital letter 'Z' is made with three straight lines.

1. The first line is a horizontal line the width of the letter. This is drawn at the top of the letter.

2. The second stroke begins at the top right of the letter and angles straight down, to the left, proceeding to the bottom of the letter.

3. The third stroke is from the left juncture to right the width of the letter.

Words: ZINC, ZIG, ZAG, BRAZIL, DIZZY, DRIZZLE, FIZZ, FRAZZLE, FRIZZY, GIZZARD, GUZZLE, HAZARD, LIZARD, MIZEN, MUZZLE, NUZZLE, PLAZA, PUZZLE, WIZARD, ZEST, ZINNIA, ZIP.

Sentences: JAN DID A PUZZLE. A LIZARD SAT IN A SUNNY SPOT. SAM TURNED TILL HE WAS DIZZY. POP HAS A FIZZ. A RIVER CAN BE A HAZARD. A HOT PAN WILL SIZZLE. SAM WILL GUZZLE HIS POP.

Professor Bloomer's No-Nonsense Reading Program
Lesson 24

Z_____

_____

PICTURES TO LABEL

ZEBRA

MUZZLE

LIZARD

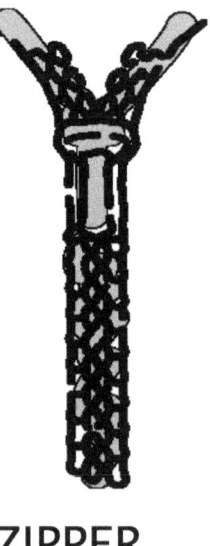
ZIPPER

WIZARD

ZINNIA

Professor Bloomer's No-Nonsense Reading Program
Lesson 24

Beginning Review: Procedure, Teachers manual Page 6-7: **(Use separate lined paper for this exercise)**

Letter/sounds /A/ /T/ /S/. /M/ /R/ /G/./F/, /W/, /R/ /N/ /U/, /H/ /J/, /L/. /C/, /I/ /V/, /K/, /B/, /O/, /Y/, /P/, /E/

the words, AFTER, BED, BEG, BELL, BEN, BEST, BET, DELL, DEN, DRESS, EGG, ELF, ELM, ELSE, END, FED, EVER, FELL, GET, GLEN, HELP, HEW, HEN, HER, JELL, LED, JELLY, LEG, LEND, LENT, JEST, LESS, JESUS, LEST, JET, LET, LINEN, KEG, MEN, MESS, MET, METAL, NECK, NEST, NET, NEVER, PEG, PEN, RED, PEST, RENT, PET, REST, SELF, SEND, SENT, SERUM, SEVEN, SET, SELL, STEM, TELL, TEN, TENSE, TEST, VERSE, SISTER, VEST, VET, WATER, WED, WENT, WERE, VERY, WELL, WEST, WET.

Introducing the Letter/sound /Z/, Procedure: Teacher's Manual page 1; **(Student Workbook page 155).**

Constructive Synthesis: Procedure: Teacher's Manual page 8; **(use separate lined paper)**

for the words ZINC, ZIG, ZAG, BRAZIL, DIZZY, DRIZZLE, FIZZ, FRAZZLE, FRIZZY, GIZZARD, GUZZLE, HAZARD, LIZARD, MIZEN, MUZZLE, NUZZLE, PLAZA, PUZZLE, WIZARD, ZEBRA, ZEST, ZINNIA, ZIP.

Pictures to Label: Procedure Teacher's Manual page 10: **(Student Workbook page 155)**.

ZEBRA, MUZZLE, LIZARD, ZIPPER, WIZARD, ZINNIA

Match and Label: Procedure, Teacher's Manual page 21, **(Student Workbook page 156)**

WIZARD, FEZ, LIZARD, TOP, PUZZLED, MUZZLE, ZINNIA, GUZZLE, ZEBRA, ZEPPELIN, ZIPPER, FIZZ

Matching words: Procedure, Teacher's Manual page 16, **(Student Workbook page 157)**

ADZ	LIZARD
FEZ	FEZ
ZINNIA	WIZARD
LIZARD	DIZZY
DIZZY	BRAZIL
DRIZZLE	GUZZLE
BRAZIL	ZINNIA
GUZZLE	ADZ
WIZARD	DRIZZLE

MATCH AND LABEL

WIZARD
FEZ
WIZARD
TOP
PUZZLED
MUZZLE
ZINNIA
GUZZLE
ZEBRA
ZEPPELIN
ZIPPER
FIZZ

Professor Bloomer's No-Nonsense Reading Program
Lesson 24

Finding word pairs and Reading aloud: Procedure Teacher's Manual page 16: **(Student Workbook page 157)**

ADZ	ZIP	**ADZ**	ZEST
LIZARD	**GIZZARD**	**GIZZARD**	HAZARD
FRAZZLE	FRIZZ	NUZZLE	**FRAZZLE**
FIZZ	**FIZZ**	PLAZA	FRIZZY
ZEST	PUZZLE	**WIZARD**	**WIZARD**
BRAZIL	PLAZA	**BRAZIL**	HAZARD
DIZZY	MUZZLE	**DIZZY**	PUZZLE
DRIZZLE	ZINNIA	BRAZIL	**DRIZZLE**
DIZZY	**ZEBRA**	ADZ	**ZEBRA**

Flash Identification: Procedure Teacher's Manual page 46: **(Student Workbook page 158)**

Letters to Flash are: **Z, S, A, O, Z, E, I, Z, D, F.**

Z	SET	SI**ZZ**LE	SIP	**Z**IP
S	MA**S**T	**S**TAR	PUZZLE	ZE**S**T
A	FR**A**ZZLE	ZINNI**A**	ZIP	**S**AND
O	PLAZA	C**O**ST	DECK	M**O**SS
Z	SEND	LI**Z**ARD	**Z**EST	VEST
E	T**E**LL	DIZZY	DICK	D**E**CK
I	L**I**ZARD	LET	ZEST	DR**I**ZZLE
Z	FELL	SEND	WI**Z**ARD	PLA**Z**A
D	PLAZA	BRAZIL	HAZAR**D**	**D**IZZY
F	HAZARD	**F**RAZZLE	**F**RIZZ	NUZZLE

Sounds in words: Procedure Teacher's Manual page 32: **(Student Workbook page 158)**

The sequence of Letter/sounds in this lesson is as follow /S/, /Z/, /N/, /F/, /V/, /Z/, /D/, /T/, /P/.

/S/	ZIP	**S**IP	ZIP	LI**S**T	**S**IZZLE
/Z/	PLANT	PLA**Z**A	COST	BRA**Z**IL	AFTER
/N/	ZEST	**N**EST	FIZZ	DICK	ZI**N**C
/F/	**F**IN	ZIP	LIZARD	SEND	**F**RAZZLE
/V/	PUZZLE	**V**EST	HA**V**E	ZEST	**V**ISIT
/Z/	SI**ZZ**LE	GI**ZZ**ARD	SANTA	NEST	WI**Z**ARD
./D/	ZEST	HAZAR**D**	BEN**D**	WIZAR**D**	BRAZIL
/T/	LIZARD	LE**T**	ZES**T**	DRIZZLE	**T**ELL
/P/	ZINNIA	ZI**P**	SAND	**P**LAZA	COST

WHAT IS THIS?   CAN YOU MAKE IT BETTER?

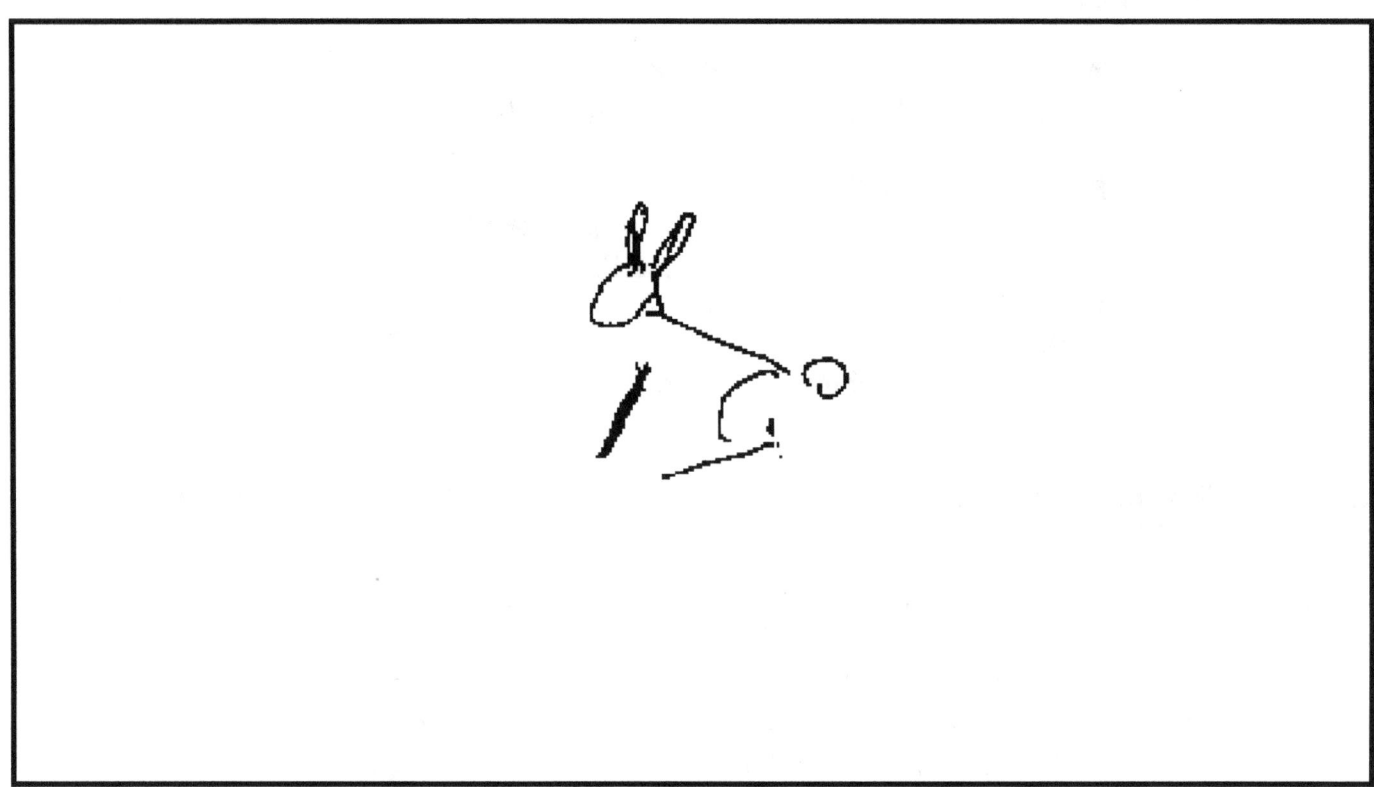

CAN YOU DRAW IT BETTER DOWN HERE?

Professor Bloomer's No-Nonsense Reading Program
Lesson 24

Dictation: Procedure, Teacher's Manual page 16, **(Student Workbook page 158)**

Letter/soundS, /A/, /T/, /S/, /M/, /R/, /G/, /F/, /W/, /R/, /N/, /U/, /H/, /J/, /L/, /C/, /I/, /V/, /K/, /B/, /O/, /Y/, /P/, /E/, /Z/,.

and the WORDS, ZINC, ZIG, ZAG, BRAZIL, DIZZY, DRIZZLE, FIZZ, FRAZZLE, FRIZZY, GIZZARD, GUZZLE, HAZARD, LIZARD, MIZEN, MUZZLE, NUZZLE, PLAZA, PUZZLE, WIZARD, ZEBRA, ZEST, ZINNIA, ZIP.

Picture completion: Procedure Teacher's Manual page 46: **(Student Workbook page 159)**

How many words can you make? Procedure Teacher's Manual page 32: **(Student Workbook page 160)**

The Letter/sounds are G, Z, S, L, A, R, N, B, I, E, W, U.

Phrases to Read Aloud and Write: Procedure Teacher's Manual page 37-38: **(Student Workbook page 160)** **(Use separate lined paper for this exercise)**

SAM CAN GUZZLE A POP._____
TOM'S DOG HAS A MUZZLE._____
A LIZARD SAT IN HOT SAND._____
DAN SAW A ZEBRA IN A HUT._____
SOME WATER WAS IN A ZINC TUB._____
A ZINC SINK DID NOT COST A LOT._____
BART RAN ZIG, ZAG._____
TOM HAD SOME ZINC ORE._____
A ZEBRA RUNS ON LAND._____
NED WAS DIZZY AND FELL OFF A CLIFF._____
JACK AND JILL RAN ZIG ZAG UP A BIG HILL._____
AN ADZ CAN CUT A LOG._____

Professor Bloomer's No-Nonsense Reading Program
Lesson 24

Completing Phrases: Procedure Teacher's Manual page 38-39: **(Student Workbook page 161)**

SALLY'S BOTTLE OF PO**P** HAS A FI**ZZ**. (P, ZZ)
JAN DI**D** A PU**ZZ**LE. (D, ZZ)
A **R**IVER CAN BE A HA**Z**ARD. (R, Z)
SAM **W**ILL **G**UZZLE HIS PO**P**. (W, G, P)
AN AD**Z** CAN C**U**T A LOG. (Z, U)
A **Z**EBRA RUNS ON LAN**D**. (Z, D)

Picture Phrases: Procedure, Teacher's Manual page 16, **(Student Workbook page 161-162)**

ZEPPLIN, PRETZELS, WIZARD, ZEBU, LIZARD, ZEBRA, FLYING LIZARD, FEZ.

How many sentences can you make? Procedure, Teacher's Manual page 99, **(Student Workbook page 162) (Use separate lined paper for this exercise)**

CAT, LIZARD, A, RUN, PICK, WARM, NED, IS, BRAZIL, DAN, RUNS, AT, IN, BED, UNDER, ROCK, PLAZA, SAT, ZEBRA, WIZARD, WAND, RAT HAS, WAS, UNDER, OVER, NO, WAS, NOT, TO, THE, UP, DOWN, IT.

Special Review:

Letter: Review for sound and shape: S.

Words: SAG, ZAG, SIZZLE, ZEST

Comment: There may be some difficulty in teaching the difference between the S and the Z. It Is also probable that there will be some reversals of S when the children first meet Z. This problem can best be avoided by pointing out the differences,

PICTURE PHRASES

Professor Bloomer's No-Nonsense Reading Program
Lesson 243

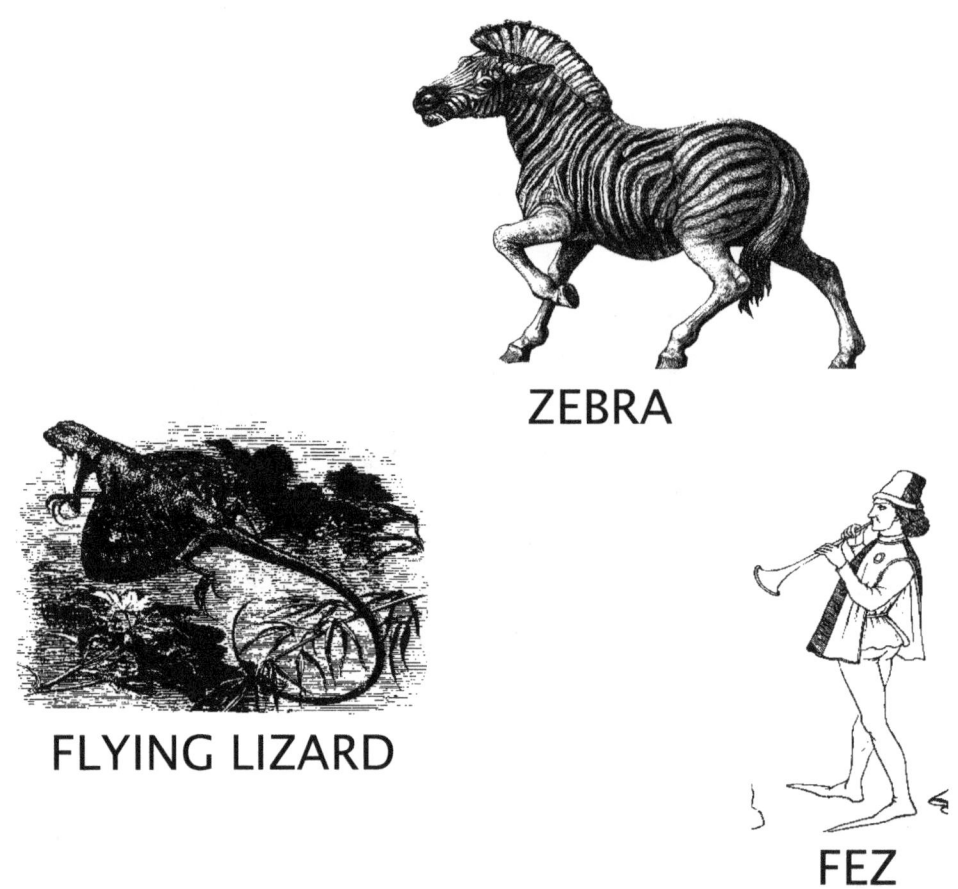

ZEBRA

FLYING LIZARD

FEZ

Comment: Read the story **AT THE ZOO** in Professor Bloomer's No-Nonsense Phonetic Reader for more practice.

Professor Bloomer's No-Nonsense Reading Program
Lesson 25

Lesson 25 The Letter/sound /X/

Purpose: Unit XXVI introduces the Letter/sound /X/ as in AX and related words. The unit is a final preparatory unit before most of the time is devoted to reading, emphasizes the skill of using word in the context of short stories.

Timing Note: This lesson should take at least THREE sessions preferably separated by a whole day. Teachers should judge by the quality of the learner's responses whether to continue on or to rehearse for a longer period. Resting time between learning sessions for consolidation of learning is essential. Remember to start each session with a Review. Time is not important, Quality is.

Letter/sound. /X/. /X/ as in AX Sounds like the two Letter/sounds /K/ and /S/ merged,. /X/ is formed by stopping a column of air with the tongue high in the roof of the mouth, and releasing it. The release is accompanied with a movement of the tongue close to the roof of the mouth just behind the upper front teeth. The column of air is continued and forced between the tip of the tongue and the teeth. /X/ is not voiced

L.etter Formation **X**
'X' The capital letter 'X' is made of two straight lines

    1. The first stroke starts at the top of the letter and angles down to the right at about 60 degrees

    2. The second stroke starts at the top of the letter, a letter's width to the right and angles down to the left at about 60 degrees to cross the first line in the middle of the letter.

Words: AX, EXCEL, EXIT, HEX, LAX, BOX, FIX, FLAX, FOX, DEXTERITY, MIX, NEXT, OX, RELAX, TAX, TAXI, OXEN, REX TEXT, TOXIN, VEX, WAX.

Sentences: DAD WILL FIX A FLAT. A FOX LIVES IN A DEN. AN OX DRAGGED A SLED. SAM MIXED SAND AND DIRT. WATER AND WAX WILL NOT MIX. MOM WILL MIX AN EGG NOG.

Procedure: The letter X is introduced following the procedure of Unit XIX.

Beginning Review: Procedure, Teachers manual Page 6-7: **(Use separate lined paper for this exercise)**

    Letter/sounds /A/ /T/ /S/. /M/ /R/ /G/./F/, /W/, /R/ /N/ /U/, /H/ /J/, /L/. /C/, /I/ /V/, /K/, /B/, /O/, /Y/, /P/, /E/, /Z/ **and the words,** ZINC, ZIG, ZAG, BRAZIL, DIZZY, DRIZZLE, FIZZ, FRAZZLE, FRIZZY, GIZZARD, GUZZLE, HAZARD, LIZARD, MIZEN, MUZZLE, NUZZLE, PLAZA, PUZZLE, WIZARD, ZEBRA, ZEST, ZINNIA, ZIP

Professor Bloomer's No-Nonsense Reading Program
Lesson 25

Introducing the Letter/sound /X/ Procedure Teacher's Manual page 1: **(Student Workbook page 163)**

The Letter/sound /X/ as in FOX

Constructive Synthesis: Procedure: Teacher's Manual page 8; **(Use separate lined paper for this exercise)**

Words AX, EXCEL, EXIT, HEX, LAX, BOX, FIX, FLAX, FOX, DEXTERITY, MIX, NEXT, OX, RELAX, TAX, TAXI, OXEN, REX TEXT, TOXIN, VEX, WAX.

Pictures to Label: Procedure Teacher's Manual page 10: **(Student Workbook page 163)**

FOX(ES), OX, OXEN, TAXI, BOX, AX

Match and Label: Procedure, Teacher's Manual page 21, **(Student Workbook page 164)**

OX, SIX, SAW, OXEN, TAXI, AX, FOX, BOX, FIX, WAX, DRAGON.

Matching words: Procedure, Teacher's Manual page 16, **(Student Workbook page 165)**

NEXT	BOX
TAX	WAX
BOX	FOX
WAX	TAX
FOX	FIX
MIX	NEXT
RELAX	MIX
FIX	RELAX

Finding word pairs and Reading Aloud: Procedure, Teacher's Manual page 16,**(Student Workbook page 165)**

EXIST	FLAX	**EXIST**	BOX
FOXY	BOX	**FOXY**	NEXT
MIX	**TAX**	**TAX**	NEXT
FOX	FLAX	EXIT	**FOX**
LAX	**BOX**	FLAX	**BOX**
FIX	RELAX	**FIX**	OX
FLICK	**NEXT**	**NEXT**	RELAX
MIX	**EXIT**	TAX	**EXIT**
OX	NEXT	BOX	**OX**

Professor Bloomer's No-Nonsense Reading Program
Lesson 25

X _____

_____

PICTURES TO LABEL

FOXES

OX

OXEN

TAXI

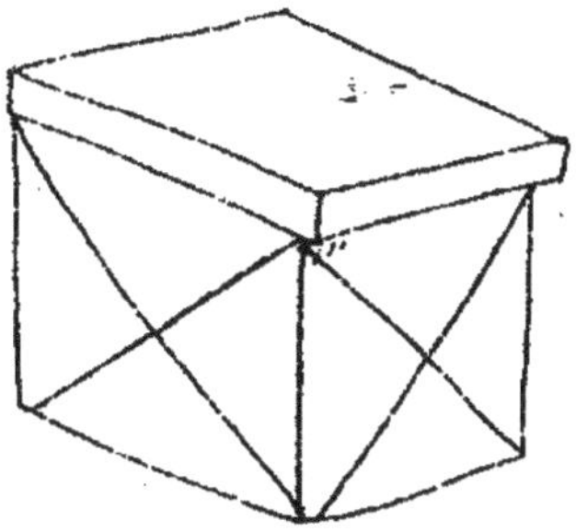

BOX

AX

213

Professor Bloomer's No-Nonsense Reading Program
Lesson 25

MATCH AND LABEL

OX
SIX
SAW
OXEN
TAXI
AX
FOX
BOX
FIX
WAX

OXEN

FOX

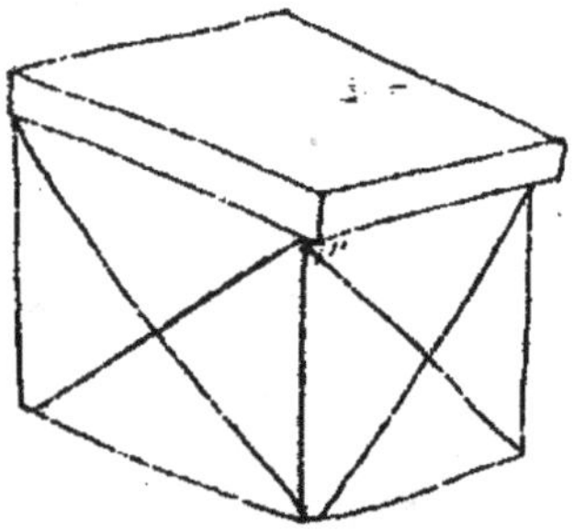

BOX

AX

FIX

TAXI

WAX

DRAGON

OX

SAW

SIX

Professor Bloomer's No-Nonsense Reading Program
Lesson 25

Flash Identification: Procedure Teacher's Manual page 46: **(Student Workbook page 166)**

Letters to Flash are: **X, F, S, X, V, W, X, Y.**

X	FO**X**	WAS	O**X**EN	SIZZLE
F	**F**OX	EXIT	BOX	**F**LAX
S	MI**SS**	NE**S**T	LAX	WAX
X	E**X**IT	ZEST	TEST	SA**X**
V	OXEN	O**V**EN	SAW	LAX
W	FIX	NEST	**W**AS	TEXAS
X	WA**X**	BOSS	FO**X**	WAS
Y	FOX**Y**	BOX	BO**Y**	LAX

Sounds in words: Procedure Teacher's Manual page 32: **(Student Workbook page 166)**

The sequence to use in this lesson is as follow: /X/, /S/, /Z/, /X/, /V/, /W/, /X/, /Y/, /R/.

/X/	MI**X**	TE**X**AS	MISS	NE**X**T	LA**X**
/S/	WAX	BO**SS**	FOX	WA**S**	OXEN
/Z/	SI**ZZ**LE	EXIST	**Z**EST	TEST	SAX
/X/	TEST	BO**X**	E**X**IST	BOY	PYRE**X**
/V/	OXEN	O**V**EN	SAW	**V**AST	MISS
/W/	LAX	FLA**W**	PIXY	LA**W**	RELAX
/X/	WA**X**	FI**X**	NEST	WAS	TE**X**AS
/Y/	FOX**Y**	BOX	BO**Y**	LAX	WAX**Y**
/R/	NEXT	**R**ELAX	MIX	EXIT	TAX

Dictation: Procedure Teacher's Manual page 16: **(Student Workbook page 166)**
(Use separate lined paper for this exercise)

Letter/soundS /A/ /T/ /S/. /M/ /R/ /G/./F/, /W/, /R/ /N/ /U/, /H/ /J/, /L/. /C/, /I/ /V/, /K/, /B/, /O/, /Y/, /P/, /E/, /Z/ , /X/,
and the WORDS, AX, EXCEL, EXIT, HEX, LAX, BOX, FIX, FLAX, FOX, DEXTERITY, MIX, NEXT, OX, RELAX, TAX, TAXI, OXEN, REX TEXT, TOXIN, VEX, WAX.

Professor Bloomer's No-Nonsense Reading Program
Lesson 25

WHAT IS THIS?   CAN YOU MAKE IT BETTER?

CAN YOU DRAW IT BETTER DOWN HERE?

Professor Bloomer's No-Nonsense Reading Program
Lesson 25

Picture completion: Procedure Teacher's Manual page 46: **(Student Workbook page 167)**

How many words can you make? Procedure Teacher's Manual page 32: **V(Student Workbook page 168)**

The Letter/sounds are: I. F. O. X, S, L, A, B, T, E, V, N, W, Z.

Phrases to Read Aloud and Write: Procedure Teacher's Manual page 37-38: **(Student Workbook page 168) (Use separate lined paper for this exercise)**

JACK CAN FIX A FLAT._____
MAMA IS VEXED._____
A FOX IS FOXY_____
NAN CAN MIX A SALAD._____
DAD WAS IN A TAXI._____
TOM PUT SOME CANDY IN A BOX_____
BERT CAN RELAX IN HIS BED._____
THE JELLY JAR HAD A WAX TOP._____
LINEN IS MADE OF FLAX._____
WIZARD CAN MIX A TOXIN ._____
AN ANT CANNOT EXIST IN A BOX._____
TOM FED AN OX SOME BRAN._____
BESS CAN PRESS HER DRESS NEXT._____
GAS HAS A TAX ON IT._____
MAMA AND DAD HAD SIX BOYS._____
SALLY HAS A WAX DOLL._____

Completing Phrases: Procedure Teacher's Manual page 38-39: **(Student Workbook page 169)**

A **F**OX LIVES IN A **D**EN. (F, D)
MOM WILL MI**X** AN **E**GG NOG. (X, E)
BERT CAN RELA**X** IN HIS **B**ED. (X, B)
A **F**OX IS FOX**Y**. (F, Y)
A **J**ELLY **J**AR CAN HAVE A **W**AX TOP. (J, W)
TOM **F**ED AN **O**X SOME GRASS. (F, O)

Professor Bloomer's No-Nonsense Reading Program
Lesson 25

PicturesPhreses: Procedure, Teacher's Manual page 16, **(Student Workbook page 169-70)**

> LYNX, A BUNNY IN A BOX. A BOXER, MUSK OX, MEN BOXING, A FOX AND A CAT. AN OX, A BOX AND SOME FOXES. DOGS RUN AFTER A FOX. A DOG SAT ON A BOX.

How many sentences can you make? Procedure, Teacher's Manual page 99, **(Student Workbook page 170) (Use separate lined paper for this exercise)**

> BOX. SAT, ON, A, UP, FIX, BOY, IN, FOX, OF, WAX, ,CAN, RAN, ROCK, MILL, HILL, AFTER, LIZARD, OX, RELAX, DAN, OVEN, EXIT, TEXAS, MIX, JAM, BED, TAXI, UNDER, NO, WAS, NOT, TO, THE, A, IN, UP, DOWN, AT..

Special Review:
Letters: Review for sound: /S/, /X/, /Z/.

Words: SIX, EXIST, SAX, TEXAS.

Letters: Review for shape: V, W, Y.

Words: VEX, FOXY, WAXY.

Words: S words: LAX-ALAS, TEXT-TEST, BOX-BASS, MIX-MISS, NEXT-NEST, WAX-WAS.
   V words: VEX, OXEN-OVEN, LAX-LAVA.
   W words: HEX-HEW, LAX-LAW, SAX-SAW, FLAX-FLAW.
   Y words: PICKY, FOXY, WAXY, PYREX, BOX-BOY.

PICTURE PHRASES

LYNX

RABBIT IN A BOX

BOXER

MUSK OX

MEN BOXING

Professor Bloomer's No-Nonsense Reading Program
Lesson 25

A CAT AND A FOX

DOGS AFTER A FOX

AN OX GOT IN A BOX

A DOG ON A BOX

Comment: Read the story **SIX FOXES AND AN OX** in Professor Bloomer's No-Nonsense Phonetic Reader for more practice._____

A Short History of Professor Bloomer's No-Nonsense Reading Program for Young Learners

Remedial Reading in Wichita

As a young graduate student I focused my studies on the science of how people learn, the basic science underlying all Education. The instructor for the reading methods class at the City University of Wichita, Kansas went on sabbatical. I was hired to fill in for him and teach reading methods to prospective teachers . I began to study for the class. As a learning scientist the reading textbook made no sense. There was a lot of confusing language and procedures that didn't appear to me to help children learn to read. I decided to apply the principles of learning science to teaching reading

I knew absolutely nothing about Education, but I had studied a great deal about human learning. I knew that any successful teaching program should be simple. It should give little opportunity for confusing the learner. It should be as regular or consistent as possible. The student should be as active a participant in the learning as possible. Most important an effective beginning reading program should teach the learner the processes of reading, not just the memorization of words.

With these principles in mind, I devised a small manual with the help of my students. To help learners avoid confusion, we developed the mathematical tables of letter shape discriminability, to determine the clearest order of presentation for capital letters. I asked classes in speech pathology to rank Letter/sounds on their similarity. We used the similarity ratings to develop a mathematical scale of Letter/sound discriminability. Using these tables we were able to arrange effective sequences of letter sounds and shapes designed to avoid confusion. We used only capital letters to avoid the confusion of letter similarity. We selected only phonetically regular words that developed from our teaching sequence of Letter/sounds. Developing our teaching guide took us about five weeks. What to do for the rest of the semester?

Learning Disabilities would not be discovered for another twenty years. But there were plenty of poor readers in the schools. I arranged for my students to go into schools to work with some of these poor readers. My students were so successful I had several principals clamoring for more help with their poor readers. We eventually developed a successful campus clinic for helping children overcome their reading problems.

The First Classroom Test

I decided to try the program in a classroom. I approached several of those school principals who were so pleased with my students and was turned down by every one.

> "It's not what we do" they said.

> "We don't do phonetics," they said.

> "Our teachers are using the Whole Word Method" they said.

> "We like reading for meaning," they said.

Undaunted I continued to approach school principals. Finally In a small town on the outskirts of Wichita I found a willing principal.

"We have just finished our mid-year testing," she said. "I have a first year, first grade teacher whose children scored far below my veteran, first grade teacher. She's so bad, I am going have to fire her at the end of the year. You can have her"

I thanked the principal, and I took my little manual down the hall to that first grade teacher's room. She seemed to welcome the help and said our manual made sense to her. I came back weekly to watch her progress and give her support for the rest of the year. The children progressed rapidly. One little boy who had a speech disorder told her he felt so much better now that all the children had to learn to say things right. When the final end of the year test results came back, my reject teacher's class performed better than the more experienced seven year teacher. Her job was saved!! Some twenty odd years later, following a talk I gave at the International Reading Association conference, she reintroduced herself. She was nearly ready to retire from teaching and was still using that little manual.

Experimental trials at Geneseo
A few years later when teaching learning at Geneseo State Teachers College in upstate New York, I was approached by some students in the summer emergency teacher certification program for help. They were to take two summer courses and start classroom teaching in the fall. They would finish their certification on Saturdays over the next two years. One of the courses was my Human Learning course, the other was Educational Methods..

My students complained they weren't learning any thing in Educational Methods. I promised to see what I could do.

I went to visit their Educational Methods class. The class was a group of children in for summer remedial work for the prospective teachers to practice with. As I approached the classroom I heard a child screaming. Entering, I saw one little boy repeatedly beating another boy on the head with one of those heavy metal Tonka toys. "You," I yelled, "Stop that!"   The child stopped.

"What do you mean, interrupting my class?" Screeched the instructor, a brand new faculty member.

"You should try to get your classroom under control." I retorted

It was then I noticed all twenty of the students from my learning class sitting in the back of the room doing nothing. The presumed instructor was sitting at her desk on the front of the room with the New York Times opened on her desk. No one was interacting with the twenty children, who were doing whatever they pleased.

This was during peak of Progressive Education, the extreme Freudian non-inhibition, "Freedom of Expression" educational fad. The notion was, if you just waited the children were supposed to come to the "Teachable Moment." To do other than wait for this magical moment was to frustrate the poor little children, and give them deep seated conflicts which would take years of psychoanalysis to purge from their unconscious Ids. It was clear, three weeks into a six week session that the "Teachable Moment" was unlikely to arise in that classroom.

I offered to spend time each afternoon to help my students learn about the classroom. We started, obviously, with the most important; techniques to gain control of a class so the children would pay attention and stay focused. We proceeded through housekeeping tasks, little tasks like lining up, moving down the hall, getting their outer wear hung up, and keeping the class register. All of which had been ignored in their "free range" educational methods class. When it came to teaching itself, I outlined simple techniques based on learning principles for the "Three R's." I included the Constructive Synthesis reading method I had first designed in Kansas.

Three of the teachers offered to try my reading manual. I visited each of their principals who agreed to participate in an experiment comparing my method with the then popular "Basal Reading Method." That summer I designed a pupil's workbook to follow the teacher's manual and spent the rest of the summer mimeographing these for the children's use.

In the fall I visited each classroom weekly to keep tabs on their progress. My teachers' major concern was that they were not doing what every other teacher was doing.

"Miss Jones's class is reading in pre primer books already, and we don't have any" We're falling behind."

It required considerable persuasion on my part to keep them from rushing headlong into the collegial comfort of the basal reader program. Their concerns spurred me to write some phonetically consistent stories, carefully paced to go along with the reading program. By January my teachers had finished the first years' section of Professor Bloomer's Reading program.

"What shall we do now? "

"Read those primers from the basal program."

The children read their primers in less than a week. The basal reading classes had required nearly two months.

"What shall we do now?"

"Have the children read the first reader from the basal program."

The children spent the better part of two weeks on that first reader. The basal classes had required three months for the first reader.
"We've finished the first reader. What do we do now?"

"Read the second reader from your basal reading program."

By the end of February the children in these classes had completed not only Professor Bloomers Reading Program, but also all the work the basal program offered. The other classes would not complete the basal program till June.

"We've finished the basal reader program. What shall we do next?"
"Just have the children read. Take them to the library to take out books, whatever you can find, any children's books, let them read."

Results:
At the end of the year we administered standardized tests to our three classes of Professor Bloomer's Reading Program and the thirty other basal reader control classes in their same school systems. The average for Professor Bloomers Reading Program for Young Readers was a grade level equivalent of 3.23. Over half or the Professor Bloomer's Reading Program children scored over third grade level at the end of first grade! The average score for the basal reader controls classes was grade level 2.43. Professor Bloomer's classes had an eight month advantage. Further, no single child in Professor Bloomer's program scored below the grade level of 2.43, the average for the basal reader whole language classes. Of the children taught by the standard "dick & Jane program, twenty-two percent of those basal reader children were still reading at kindergarten level. They had not even achieved at beginning first grade level. In essence fifty percent of the basal children scored below the lowest of the Professor Bloomer's children. None of the Professor Bloomer's children were left behind. We ran this experiment for two years with similar results. More than half the Professor Bloomer's children had perfect scores on the grade appropriate tests.

Teachers who participated in our trial reading program were often pressured by their administrators and peers to try more conventional programs so everyone would be doing the same thing. One by one they tried one or another of these commercial programs and experienced their first failures. Much to the consternation of their colleagues two of them returned to Professor Bloomer's Reading Program. One teacher I kept in contact with over her twenty-seven years of teaching. She used Professor Bloomer's program in defiance of fellow teachers and administrators who wanted everything uniform. The administration countered by sending her all the weakest students identified in kindergarten. In spite of this, her class's average reading scores exceeded all the other twenty-seven first grades in the system each year. She suffered her single learner failure in all her twenty-seven years of teaching, and that year she gave in to peer pressure and tried a "Similar" commercial program.

I, of course, was delighted by the results. I grew up during the depression years when one of the common myths was "Build a better mouse-trap than your neighbor, and the world will beat a path to your door."

The aftermath

I had built that better mouse-trap, a "no failure" reading program. I wrote a couple of articles for the scientific journals. The world did not respond. I wrote a letter to a major publisher. No response, except the usual form letter "Thank you for considering us, your project does not fit our publishing plans." The publishing mythology of the time was you only wrote a proposal to only one publisher at a time. I presume that was to prevent you from having any bargaining leverage. Over time I worked my way through a list and wrote to some 150 publishers, every one I could imagine might have the least interest in reading. The results were negative to none.

My students and I continued to use my reading program over the years. It worked exceptionally well with remedial readers, and students with learning disabilities, many of whom learned to read, and then had to fight to get "undiagnosed" from special education. We converted this same constructive synthesis phonetic model into program for children from low SES, a Braile reading program for the blind, a Spanish reading program for Latin America, a tutorial program for adolescents non-readers in the Job Corps, and a Reading/Typing progam for first and second graders which reduced the Special Education roles by sixty-seven percent. All of these programs were far superior to the programs of commercial publishers.

www.ingramcontent.com/pod-product-compliance
Lightning Source LLC
Chambersburg PA
CBHW081454040426
42446CB00016B/3239